BEAUTY, TRUTH AND GRACE

Pageant Coaching to Win
On Stage and in Life

Praise for Alycia Darby

"Hands-down best Pageant podcast out there. Alycia is truly knowledgeable and beyond inspiring. It really gets you into the right mindset." ~ Izzy

"Alycia goes in depth on every topic you could possibly think of that's pageant related. Super informative!" ~ Erin

"Alycia is a fabulous coach. I've learned more about myself than I had with any other coach that I met with face to face." ~ Rita

"Her coaching is built on the basic tenets of good teaching. Her techniques are backed by science, augmented by her proven record of success and topped off by her unique personality and perspective that only Alycia can offer." ~ Helen

"Alycia is nothing short of fantastic. Her tips, techniques, support and encouragement is a must for success." ~ Susan

"Alycia is hands-down one of the most inspirational women in my life." ~ Lexie

"The knowledge I have gained transformed my platform into something so big so beyond me that not only did it give me the competitive edge I needed in the pageant, but now I will positively affect more people than I ever dreamed possible!" ~ Candice

"Alycia changed my life! Literally! I highly recommend her." ~ Lauryn

"I feel so much more confident! Looking forward to gracing the stage with confidence, fierce determination, and of course, success." ~ Mallory

"Working with Alycia really boosted my level of confidence. I'm extremely grateful to Alycia for helping my dreams become a reality." ~ Dixie

BEAUTY, TRUTH AND GRACE

Pageant Coaching to Win
On Stage and In Life

ALYCIA DARBY ZIMNOCH

This book is dedicated to my pageant sisters and friends around the globe who have listened to and supported Win A Pageant on iTunes and YouTube. You are dedicated to developing your gifts, honing your skills, and leaving a legacy of love on stage and in life. You, my dear, are the light of the world. This book is for you.

INTRODUCTION

I believe in dreams. I think a dream is a whisper to our heart from God of what he has in store for us as unique and wonderful creations. Dreams are a foreshadowing of what's to come, but we have to chase the dream to make it a reality. Every dream I've chased has led me to something unexpected and amazing, more than I could have asked for or imagined. It's not easy to chase your dream, but achieving your dream allows you to contribute to the world in your unique way and live your best life.

Dreams aren't easy to chase. They don't just lie down for the taking; you have to overcome a lot to make them a reality. It breaks my heart when a woman doesn't chase her dreams. Every unfulfilled dream leaves a hole in the story of our world. It remains an empty opportunity until she finally gains the courage to go for it.

As a pageant coach, I get to participate in a lot of dreams. I believe it's my job as a woman's coach to keep her aligned with her vision and motivated to chase her dream. It's fun to guide her through the long maze of twists, valleys, and mountains on the way to her ultimate goal.

I've been coaching pageant women for over ten years. I love helping women develop transformative platforms, confidently rock their interview, radically change their communities, and leave a lasting legacy with their pageant titles. I competed in pageants for over a decade throughout the United States in local, state, and national competitions. I discovered what worked and what didn't through my own experience, and that of my clients around the world. After many years, I finally discovered a pattern of success, a strategy that worked over and over. My clients began to win their pageants and impact the world in huge ways.

I love having a coach. I've hired coaches to help me succeed in nearly every area of my life including fitness, business, dance, finances, public speaking, marriage, personal development, hosting, pageantry, modeling, and podcasting. I believe the best coach is the person who tells us the honest truth and delivers it with poetic beauty and the utmost grace.

In the summer of 2015, my friend John coached me into chasing my dream. John is a podcaster who created a step-by-step online program to help people launch podcasts all over the world. He's living his dream now after chasing it for over five years. He knows it isn't easy, but it's worth it.

I was telling John about a dream I'd had for several months. I wanted to start a podcast where I would share my winning pageant techniques for free each week on iTunes. The pageant industry lacked coaches that told the truth about what it takes to win without sugar coating it or being down right mean. I believed this podcast could radically change the pageant industry and influence more women to achieve the dream God had for them. When I told John I hoped he'd compliment my idea and maybe give me a high five.

Instead, he bluntly asked, "So why haven't you launched it yet?"

"Uh, I don't know," I admitted.

"I do," he said in a matter-of-fact tone. "Because you've got a great idea. As long as it remains an idea, you can't fail."

He was right. It was a great idea, but an idea is still just a dream until you start chasing it. He wasn't blaming me or shaming me. He wasn't pointing out problems without providing solutions. He wasn't being mean and he certainly wasn't sugar coating anything. He was stating the truth with beauty and grace to motivate me to turn my dream into a reality. This is excellent coaching.

Within hours, I joined his online program. A few weeks later, the program helped me launch my podcast, Win A Pageant. Within the first two months, the podcast appeared at the top of the iTunes "New and Noteworthy" list and has remained the #1 Pageant Podcast on iTunes since its creation in 2015. It has grown to over 100 episodes and gains thousands of listeners each month. The Win A Pageant podcast is directly responsible for coaching women to win their pageants and achieve their dreams all over the world. They listen while they're getting ready for school, at the gym, walking to class, or in their car on the way to work. My podcast dream is now a reality!

This book is another dream come true for me, and I've designed it to position you to achieve your dream too. I've compiled the podcast trainings from Win A Pageant in an organized way. Each chapter contains the trainings that pertain to a specific topic and build on one another for full comprehension. Each of the trainings is marked by its episode number 1-100. You can listen to the individual episode on our website, by visiting the link below each lesson title.

In the first few chapters, we discuss the preparation process of how to position yourself for competition and cultivate the mindset of a winner. You'll be guided through the creation of your platform, communication during your interview, even how to stand out from your competition. You'll discover how to maintain your energy during pageant week and be the best titleholder they've ever seen. This book is designed as a front-to-back training manual to coach you through your pageant competition and as an go-to resource for wisdom on particular areas. When you bump into a wall and need specific advice, you can quickly flip to a chapter and get actionable advice to apply immediately to competition and to life. Pageantry parallels life. You'll find that the coaching you receive in this book can be applied to other areas of your life.

To guide your training as you read, I've created a downloadable guidebook with the activities and exercises that are referenced throughout this book. Download the free Beauty, Truth and Grace Guidebook at: WinAPageant.com/Guide.

God has been whispering a dream on the inside of your heart. He's got something surprising and amazing prepared for you. It's your job to go all in and chase it. When you chase what God has prepared for you, He divinely intervenes to make dreams become a reality. My hope is that you'll start at the beginning of this book and apply each lesson so you will be positioned to win your pageant and fulfill the dream God whispered to your heart.

As you read, please share your insights and wins on social media using #BeautyTruthAndGrace or #WinAPageant. God gave you a dream. Chase it with beauty, truth and grace. Let's win a pageant!

Get the Guidebook
Download for Free at:
WinAPageant.com/Guide

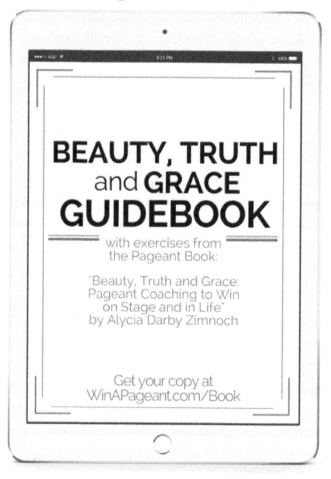

3: Becoming the Most Beautiful Contestant

Most people believe that the contestant who is the "most beautiful" wins the pageant. I agree. Most people also believe that beauty is the same as physical attractiveness. That's where they're wrong. While attractiveness is an element of the experience of beauty, it is not the only aspect that creates a beautiful experience.

According to Wikipedia, "beauty is a characteristic of a person, animal, place, object or idea that provides a perceptual experience of pleasure or satisfaction." It goes on to say that "the experience of beauty often involves an interpretation of some entity as being in balance and harmony with nature, which may lead to feelings of attraction and emotional well being."

You don't have to be gorgeous to win a pageant. The winner is the woman who is best able to create a perceptual experience of pleasure and satisfaction for her judges and audience. After all, *beauty is in the eye of the beholder.*

Imagine scrolling through Instagram and landing on a stunningly beautiful feed. You can't help but click on all the images. You're drawn in. You feel good about yourself. You feel completely connected, pleased, and inspired. It's beautiful.

Think about a time when you tasted a delicious food or drink. It melted in your mouth. You salivated for more. You were completely engulfed in the experience of the taste. You felt calmed, centered, delighted, and satisfied. It's beautiful.

I grew up on a 100-acre farm in Pennsylvania. I learned to ride my dad's four-wheeler (the city kids called them "quads") when I was in junior high. Any time I had a downer day, I'd ride it out into the trails in our backwoods, splashing through the mud pits with the sound of the engine drowning out my thoughts. When I got deep enough, I'd stop somewhere, turn off the engine, and lay on my back over the seat.

I'd breathe the clean air, watch the birds in the trees, and listen for animals walking through the brush. It was beautiful.

In her book "Captivating," Stacey Eldridge discusses a woman's innate desire to feel beautiful. She writes, "Nature is not primarily functional, it is primarily beautiful, which is to say beauty is in and of itself a great and glorious good, something that we need to indulge in daily doses of."

To better understand the experience one can have as a judge or audience member, let's look at the beautiful experience of Cirque de Soleil. If you've been to a show, you may recognize the feeling of wonder you experience as you sit on the edge of your seat with eyes wide open and constant smile of amazement as you watch the performers balance, swing, contort, climb, and fly flawlessly around the stage. Even the music, the lights, and the costumes all coincide to bring the experience to life. It's beautiful!

As a counter example, let's consider an amateur high school cheerleading show or dance recital. You know what I'm talking about. The kind that you are slouching in your chair, covering your eyes, flinching, cringing, wondering if they are going to drop the flyer and hoping they don't try anything too dangerous. Your cortisol levels are through the roof with fear that you're about to witness something terrible. It's not a good experience, no matter how gorgeous the costumes and performers are.

Beauty pageants celebrate the experience of beauty. All of the elements of beauty are considered. The costumes, lights, music, confidence, technical execution, individual attitude, and personal communication – everything must be well orchestrated to provide a pleasing and satisfactory experience that your judge will describe as beautiful. When you're on stage as a pageant contestant, you must carry yourself with calmness, grace, and confidence so your audience can relax and enjoy being in your presence. You must communicate with love. You must demonstrate self-value by presenting your body, hair, makeup and wardrobe at its very best.

You have the power to allow others to experience your beauty everywhere you go. When you're on stage competing in a pageant, at an appearance, or in your interview room, I want you to think about how you can deliver a pleasurable experience to those around you. Say things that will make them feel pleased with you and with themselves. Help them to easily understand you. Ensure that they feel at peace in your presence.

May the most beautiful woman win.

7: 12 Tips to Display Charisma like James Bond

You've heard this a million times, "She's got it!" It's the "It Factor," the attractive quality that someone exudes which makes you want to be near them, befriend them, or perhaps choose them for the title or a promotion. You know *it* when you see *it*. So…what is *"it"*? It's *Charisma*! Charisma is a unique combination of characteristics, which allow an individual to standout in a crowd, appeal to an audience, and grab the attention of judges and others.

It's no secret that charisma has the power to persuade. My dad loved the James Bond series, so I've seen all the movies dating back to the 60's, multiple times. Bond, also known as Agent 007, is one of the most charismatic characters in TV history. His charm even attracts many of his enemies and he makes it look easy.

Charisma is something that anyone can exude at all times. It has nothing to do with looks, education or skills. It is really more of an attitude. I've created a list of 12 specific things that can help you develop that "it factor" charisma like Bond, James Bond.

Tip #1 – Accept Yourself – the Good, the Bad, and the Ugly
Everyone has insecurities. Usually people are too concerned about their own insecurities to worry about yours. Acknowledge your own insecurities, and then get over it! Change what you can; accept what you can't with a smile.

Tip #2 – Expect Acceptance
If you expect others to accept you, they will note your presence and provide you respect. If you over-compensate and try to gain their acceptance, it will come off as needy and you will unintentionally lose their respect. Whenever you enter the interview room, a cocktail party, or a networking function, always expect to be accepted by all.

Tip #3 – Control your Attitude

Your attitude toward the world is a direct reflection of your character. Always show a pleasant look, nod politely when others talk, and smile a lot. Make others feel comfortable being around you and they will appreciate your positive attitude.

Tip #4 – Control your Emotions

Emotions are usually the result of over-dwelling on irrational thoughts. Learn what triggers your emotions (laughter, tears, and anger) and ask yourself "will this matter to me in three months?" If not, then dismiss irrationality. If it is a life-altering emotional reaction, allow yourself space and time to express your emotions productively and adjust accordingly.

Tip #5 – Dress the Part

Images help people categorize their thoughts. Actors "dress the part" when they audition for coveted roles so that the casting director will typecast them. Be intentional about choosing your image. Whether you're going to the gym or to the grand ball, dress the way you want to be perceived.

Tip #6 – Stand like a Model – All the Time

The way you feel about yourself is often the way others will feel about you. Project a positive self-image with a tall, confident posture; lengthen your back and neck, relax your facial muscles, and stand like your photo is always being taken.

Tip #7 – Simply Respond

Don't feel like you have to have an answer to every question you're asked. Be prepared to just respond naturally and reflectively. If you know yourself well, you'll be comfortable responding to any question – with or without an actual answer.

Tip #8 – Learn to Tell a Story

People tend to remember visual images better than just words. By using an anecdote to make a point, people will remember you longer and be more interested in your words.

Tip #9 – Own Your Mistakes (and Accomplishments)

Mistakes prove attempts. Admitting you were wrong (or right!) proves your wisdom. Own up to your mistakes and accomplishments by giving credit where credit is due, explaining the lessons you learned, and encouraging others to also try something new.

Tip #10 – Grow Thick Skin

Criticism is a great learning tool – whether or not the supplier means it to be. Filter all the criticism you receive to see if it is something you can learn from. If it applies, modify your behavior; if it doesn't apply, let it fly.

Tip #11 – Prepare, Prepare, Prepare!

Preparation is key to comfort, credibility, and advancement. Know the names of people you'll meet in social situations. Review key points of a topic prior to the meeting. Brace yourself for inevitable changes. Do all this in advance of the important meeting, interview, press conference, or social engagement.

Tip #12 – Be in the Moment

Busy people love to multitask, but they can seem distracted when engaging with people. Make a conscious effort to devote yourself completely to the task at hand or the people you're with before moving onto the next item on your to-do list. Taking the time to be in the moment will allow you to better connect with others, their concerns, and your purpose.

You can get a printable copy of these 12 tips to display charisma inside the Beauty, Truth and Grace Guidebook at WinAPageant.com/Guide. Print it out and hang it somewhere you can see it daily like your mirror, dresser, locker, dashboard of your car, shower caddy – wherever! If you read this through every day, I'm certain you'll start gaining electrifying charisma to win over everyone, especially the judges.

42: The 3 Things You Need to Win Your Pageant

WinAPageant.com/42

Every pageant winner has three specific things that help get her to the top: a mentor, community and self-value. I'll explain what each one is, why each is important, and how to get all three things to help you win.

Need #1 – Mentor

A mentor provides guidance, you can learn from their experience, and they can give you direct advice. A mentor is someone who has achieved the goal you're seeking and their willing to share their success secrets with you. Having a mentor allows you to learn vicariously through another's hard work. Most coaches in the pageant industry are also mentors because many have successfully gone through the pageant winning experience. But a mentor doesn't have to be a coach. Your mentor could be your director, parent, friend, or former titleholder. She should be someone who has stood in your shoes and achieved what you're setting out to achieve. Look for someone who is a few steps or more ahead of you and who has had authentic success. The most important thing is to find someone that shares your values because their experience, guidance, and advice will be through this lens. Prioritize what is important to them. In order to feel comfortable putting their advice into action, you'll want to be sure their values are also important to you.

Need #2 – Community

Your community is your friend base and support system. These are the people you'll reach out to for general feedback, ask to vote for you online, invite to attend the pageant, and count on to cheer you on. Having a strong community ensures you are supported by the right people who truly care.

When I first started pageants, Facebook had just started and was limited to college students only. Instead of connecting with people online, I connected with family, friends, and my local community. Fortunately, the pageant that I won had a built-in pageant board of about 16 people in various companies throughout our community. These were the people I relied on for wardrobe decisions, paperwork review, voting, attending the pageant, and to pick me up when I was down. I had a group of four wonderful girlfriends and a huge family that came to the state pageant to cheer for me and celebrate me after each round of preliminary competition. After my first year competing, I became friends with the women I was competing with and we supported one another throughout the year. However, when pageant season rolled around we all needed support at the same time and that wasn't realistic from one another, so I again relied on my pageant board of directors and friends outside of pageantry.

Nowadays, there are much easier ways to gain community that will allow for a smoother pageant experience. Free community is the one you're already a part of – your friends and family, your online followers on social media, your colleagues, and classmates. There may even be Facebook, LinkedIn, or other online groups that you could join for free online or in your city, which is especially true for people who live in more urban areas. I manage a free Facebook page for women around the world called Win A Pageant. You're welcome to join us at: Facebook.com/WinAPageant.

Another option is to join a paid community. The one I support is for all the members of my coaching program called Pageant Interview Game Plan. Members of our community are from all over the United States competing in pageants at every division from teen to Mrs. at different times throughout the year. In this group, all the women are supporting one another on decisions regarding wardrobe, platform, appearances, and everything in between. Plus, I provide mentorship and coaching in the community as well. The level of commitment and communication are far greater in paid communities than free ones because the women are much more dedicated and appreciate the support of one another far more. (For details on this program, visit: Interview.WinAPageant.com)

When you're selecting a community to become a part of, look for one where the members are active, positive and uplifting, and share your core values. Remember, you'll also want to feel comfortable giving your support to the members of the community, not just taking.

Need #3 – Self Value

It's easy when starting a new hobby to lose your own identity. We often seek to mimic those around us because we want to emulate their success. Instead of losing your sense of self in order to win, the exact opposite is true. In order to win, you have to put a high value on your individual, unique characteristics. When you have a high value on who you are, all of a sudden your confidence is stronger, you stand up for yourself more, and you don't allow other people to influence you. As a titleholder, many people will want to tell you what to do, who to hang around, what you should value, and how you should be. When you have self-value, you won't let all their yakking change who you are. Instead, you'll maintain yourself because you know it is highly valuable.

When you understand your value, your choices improve. You'll be wise about how you spend your greatest resources of time, energy, and finances. We invest our time, our energy and our finances into things we see as highly valuable. The women that value themselves wisely invest their resources on things that will propel them into their calling and achieve the dream they have for their lives. They value their health, so they spend time preparing healthy meals and working out. They value their education so they surround themselves with the greatest teachers and are constantly seeking new trainings. They value their time, so they don't waste it on things that are worthless or don't matter. They spend their time, energy, and money on things that work. You are your greatest asset.

To value yourself, you need to make a mindful decision about how you'll spend your time, energy, and finances to prepare yourself to win. Allow yourself to put high worth on you, and then spend your time, your money, and your resources accordingly. If you do not show that you value yourself, then how do you expect other people to put their time, energy, and finances into you? Don't squander what you have, invest it in what you already know is valuable: you.

34: The 4 Biggest Mistakes Pageant Girls Make

WinAPageant.com/34

If you want to win, it doesn't hurt to look at what causes women to lose so you can prepare yourself to avoid the pitfalls. Every pageant loser tends to make one of these four big mistakes, which they end up regretting after the pageant.

The contestants I speak with that are ready to make a change usually need to start in one (or more) of these four areas: Action Planning, Accountability, Fear Fighters, and Bigger Vision.

Mistake #1 – No Action Plan

An action plan helps you to prioritize, it helps you to be confident in the process and make decisions quickly. It's hard to make fast decisions when you have no plan of action. The women that don't have a plan of action spend time on things that don't matter and forget about the things that do. They have no process, no priorities, and run out of time because they don't have a strategy or system to follow.
The way to avoid this mistake is by getting a tight, crystal clear, step-by-step action plan in place and outlined before your pageant. Then you have to execute all the steps in order and on time to reach your ultimate goal of winning.

Mistake #2 – Lack of Accountability

Accountability is the partnership you create that will help you to meet your goals and deadlines. Accountability ensures that you do what you commit to at your greatest level, which increases your preparedness and confidence. We need accountability even for the things we want to do. Woman that don't have a process for accountability in place end up forgetting the big goal, giving up when they get stuck, and not seeing their commitments through to the end, which is devastating to a pageant contestant. We all need accountability even for things we are highly motivated to accomplish.

For me, my mentors, coaches, and directors were helpful to hold me accountable to the things that I already said I wanted to accomplish. They helped me create realistic milestones to get toward my goal and would remind me of how badly I wanted it when I got down on myself, which happens to everyone at some point along the way.

As a coach, I hold my entire team accountable to their high standards, which allows them to achieve far more than they could on their own without that accountability.

Mistake #3 – No Fear Fighters

As you prepare for your pageant, fear will try to get in the way and keep you from being your greatest self and accomplishing the dream that God has called you to. As the pageant gets closer and closer, the voice of fear seems to get louder and louder. Having a team of "fear fighters" will help you to knock out the negative voices by speaking life into your dreams and goals based on truth and not on fear.

Fear inevitably takes out the women that don't have a group of knowledgeable, supportive, encouraging women surrounding them. They start listening to the lies that they aren't good enough or pretty enough or smart enough. They have no one to tell them otherwise and it eats up their confidence.

When you have fear fighters in your corner – people who have guided you through the process, people that lift you up and encourage your dreams – the negative voices will be extinguished like an old flame. Your fear fighters aren't just happy-talkers. You don't want someone pretending you're all that and a bag of chips. You need people that know your depth, passion, motivation, and how hard you've prepared. These people will be able to remind you of your strengths, unique qualities, and what you are made of. They are designed to speak positive truth louder than the voices of fear.

Mistake #4 – Lack of Big Vision

A big vision helps you see past the crown and into the impact that you can have and the legacy that you can create. A vision that goes

19

beyond the crown is the difference between the woman who is a titleholder that is truly making a difference and what I call a "crown chaser." A crown chaser is the type of woman that is only after the title and not the year of service. She wants to be the queen and get the prizes, but doesn't have a desire to make a difference in the lives of others. You know these women. You've probably competed with them. Sometimes they slip through the cracks, but it's rare that they win high-stakes competitions because the judges can see right through their selfishness.

Consider how you'll use this pageant as a trampoline to solve some of the greatest issues in your community. Consider the legacy you can leave that will continue to impact positive change a year, five years or ten years after you relinquish your title. The judges want to hire a woman that is prepared to leave a legacy.

33: What You Get When You Win a Pageant

When you win a pageant, you win more than just a crown, sash, and incredible prize package (and hopefully you have a really awesome prize package). You're given the gift of influence and opportunity on many different levels. I want to introduce you to five specific gifts you'll receive so that you can use them to their absolute full potential and get a lot more out of winning your pageant.

Gift #1 – Impact

Think about all the people who impact your life today: family members that you know and respect, friends that you admire, celebrities, and teachers. The reason they have impact in your life is because you give them credibility. They know something you don't or you admire certain characteristics about them. Pageantry provides immediate credibility. A huge group of people instantly admire and resect you and the number of people you impact increases. You're able to impact people on a larger scale.

I once worked with a group of girls that have a huge following on social media. If they rave about a new juice bar, suddenly everyone goes out to try it. Once a company offended them with a bad customer service experience. Out of anger, they wanted to make a nasty post on social media to turn people away from this company. They were so used to using their credibility to impact people that it was their default method, only this time they wanted to use their credibility to impact this company in a negative way. You may be tempted to use your impact negatively too. Don't do it. When you do or say nasty things, your credibility goes down. Only use your power for good, not for evil.

Gift #2 – Access

Titleholders get to do a lot of cool stuff. Really! During my ten years of pageantry, I made a personalized silver pendant from real silver, I've attended red carpet events, met celebrities, rode a tractor in a parade, met senators and representatives – all sorts of cool activities that I wouldn't have done in the same way without a title. To make the most of your upcoming year, make a list of all the incredible things that you'd like to do as the future titleholder. Put it in your calendar and figure out a way to make it happen. One year goes by quickly, so you've got to make your list before you win.

When I was competing for Miss Pennsylvania, I knew the dates for the Pittsburg Steelers football training camps. It was always right around pageant week, so I thought if I won, I'd have to quickly make a call because I'd be giving up my title at this time the following year. What do you want to do to which being a titleholder could give you access?

Gift #3 – Opportunity

Wearing a crown really helps you stand out in a crowd. This is an opportunity to take your dreams to the next level. Think beyond the joy of being a celebrity in a room and consider what you can put into motion because of increased opportunity.

When I was Miss California International, I seized the opportunity to showcase my skills as an on-camera host. As a result, I landed a professional hosting job in Santa Monica, the most saturated media market of the world.

One year zips by quickly. To make the most of it, you'll have to think about your vision five years down the road. Consider how you can use this title to create opportunities to advance your career, platform, or personal mission.

Gift #4 – Money

As a titleholder, you'll likely receive some type of monetary prize in scholarships, cash, or in-kind gifts. You'll also have the opportunity to source for sponsors and to monetize what you're already doing. Think about the things that you need, the things that others need, and how you can come together to satisfy both of those needs in a symbiotic partnership.

Let's say a new dentist opens a business for teeth whitening, but needs reviews and testimonies to help them expand. Maybe you could help them out as a teeth model and do some promotion in exchange for their services. As a titleholder, your impact is huge and that can be shared with others when it makes sense for everyone involved.

Another way of monetizing your year is to create a product associated with your Legacy Project like a book, an event, or a packet to sell through which you can raise funds for a charity or your pageant. How cool would that be? You could raise thousands of dollars by writing a really great book that blesses the customers and the charity of your choice, which then uses the money to further expand the blessing. Money is a renewable resource. It can be generated with a little creativity, some solid partnerships, and the power of a pageant title.

Gift #5 – Personal Development

In this life, we are constantly developing. Pageantry will position you in new situations, give you new experiences, train you, build you, and grow you into a new being. When you participate in the process, you can learn new skills, build deeper character and gain confidence. You'll learn to recognize your values or make shifts in the things that you're doing, your actions, and your integrity. Whether as a pageant titleholder or not, you can consider yourself fortunate when you have people in your life that are willing to put the time and effort into training you up in ways that will help you achieve your goals beyond your one year of service.

1: Top 10 Questions to Ask Before You Decide to Compete

Before deciding to enter a pageant, it's important to know what you're getting yourself into. Every pageant is different and it's a yearlong commitment, so you'll want to be educated. These 10 questions will help you to gain insights into the mind of the directors, their values, and their perspectives and to gain feedback from former titleholders to see how you may benefit (or not) from a pageant you may choose to enter.

I recommend my clients contact the director/producer of their pageant several weeks before entry forms are due in order to give you time to connect and process their answers. A word of caution: you're going to want to email these to your director…don't. A secondary reason for calling and having this candid conversation with your director is to forge a relationship. She'll know you're serious about competing and that you are professional, reliable, and wise. Be brave and pick up the phone. She'll be delighted you're professional enough to ask the right questions.

After talking with the director, reach out to several former titleholders and request a call with them as well. Your director may even refer you to one of the titleholders she's worked with in the past. Pay particular attention to her tone of voice and the feeling behind her answers. A lot is communicated in what is not said, so use your intuition and listen to the details. Of course, in addition to these questions, you should ask any other questions that come up for you.

Questions to Ask Your Pageant Director:
1. What made the last titleholder successful?
2. What held her back?
3. What qualities are you seeking in your titleholder?
4. How do you support your titleholder throughout the year?
5. What restrictions do you have (if any) on your titleholder?

Questions to Ask Former Titleholder(s):

1. What was your year like?
2. How would you have made it better?
3. What surprised you most?
4. What do you wish you would've known?
5. What is the most important skill to be successful as this titleholder?

55: Getting the Scoop from Former Titleholders

WinAPageant.com/55

Before my client commits to a pageant, I always recommend that she talk with former titleholders to best understand her experience from the past winner's perspective. With multiple perspectives, you get a stronger view of whether or not this pageant would be a good fit for you.

I did this the first time I competed in a state pageant and I learned a TON – nothing that scared me away from the pageant, but every piece of insight and advice set me up for success in my competition.

Of course, anytime you are asking for anything, even advice, from a former titleholder, you have to approach it with grace and respect. I'll give you a list of what to do and what not to do when approaching a former titleholder of your pageant.

Let's start with what not to do.

Don't expect anyone to help you. Unless you have hired her as your coach, don't expect her to tell you what to do. Instead, just gain insights from her experience.

Don't be annoying. Don't over-ask silly things or call her back 12 times because you forgot to ask something. That's annoying.

Don't be demanding. You're the one asking for help. Don't expect her to put down everything she's doing and call you immediately. Allow your request to sink in and if she wants to help, she will.

Don't give up too soon. People are busy and get distracted. If you send a Facebook message at midnight on a Friday, they may not get it until Monday or forget to respond. It's okay to follow up, respectfully.

Don't ask a current titleholder. It's less likely you'll get the real scoop from a current titleholder. When you ask a current titleholder, it's likely you'll get a rose-colored response due to contractual obligations of a titleholder currently representing a pageant.

Don't repeat what you are told. Maintain confidentiality. You want her to be honest with you, so don't gossip, twist her words, or misrepresent anything she's told you in confidence.

Now, here's what you should do.

Determine your deal breakers. Don't just enter a pageant and say, whatever happens, happens. You wouldn't just take any job you're offered. You'd first explore the benefits, challenges, and sacrifices you'd need to make. The same is true with a pageant title. Over the years my deal breakers have been the spirit of the directors, the amount of financial support provided, the travel opportunities, level of platform support that's given, and even the level of ridiculousness of the contract you'd have to sign. If they want you to sign a contract that conflicts with your morals, don't sign it. That's a deal breaker.

Do your research. Get to know her through what she does online – get to know her platform, watch her DVD, check out her YouTube channel, read her blog. Try to get as much information on your own before you reach out.

Introduce yourself. Explain why you're reaching out and be clear about your intentions. Don't act like you aren't competing or pretend you have a mutual friend or something wacky. Just be honest.

Ask thoughtful questions. Be prepared with the five questions I've mentioned in the previous lesson and any additional ones you'd like to add.

Take notes. The conversation may bring up resources, recommendations, warning, or other things that you'll want to remember. You may not be able to remember everything she says in a 20-minute conversation, so be prepared to write down notes as you talk.

Listen closely & interpret for yourself. Pay attention to not only what she says but also how she says it. This is going to be key to interpret what she tells you into meaning for you. Just because she loves one thing doesn't mean that you will. You may have a different set of values or intentions and that thing she loves may clash for you.

Look for themes. Look for themes between what each former titleholder tells you. If they all talk about how fun and supportive the director is or they send out warnings about walking on eggshells around certain people or how much money it costs to participate, or whatever – write it down so you can compare notes after you've spoken to several.

Show your gratitude. Tell her thank you for her time and for her contribution to your success. Send a thank you note or thoughtful gift to show you're grateful to her.

19: Are You Really Ready to Compete?

WinAPageant.com/19

Competition can appear to be so much fun – and it is! But it also takes a lot of commitment to truly have a great year and get the most out of it.

Preparing for any major event may require changes in your lifestyle, where you spend your time and how you prioritize your activities. When you aren't prepared, you risk losing the pageant, coming up short in your personal life, and mismanaging your resources.

With a full understanding of what you need to do in your life to position yourself to win your pageant, you'll be prepared to step into the role with full confidence. Plus, others will know they can count on you and respect you for your ability to deliver on your promises.

To better understand if you're really ready to make the changes necessary to compete and win, here is a list of 10 questions to consider before you decide to compete for your title.

1. Why do I want to compete/win? What do I hope to take away from this experience?
2. Will this pageant help me to accomplish that goal?
3. What is my goal for final placement (top 10, top 5, winner)?
4. How much time do I need to prepare?
5. What will I have to sacrifice to put in the proper effort to win?
6. What will I need in terms of partners, preparation, and finances?
7. What resources do I need to prepare?
8. If I win, what will need to change (priorities, budget, activities, location, friendships, relationships, work responsibilities)?
9. Is there anything else that will need to change?
10. Am I okay with these changes? (How does my family feel about these changes?)

Once you've gone through all of these questions, you may feel 100% ready to commit to the pageant. Or, like most of us, you may still have this one question still hanging over your head: "What will other people think of me?"

That's a scary one because we all want to feel accepted – if you decide to compete in a pageant, maybe your parents will think you're silly or your boyfriend will say something like "that's for dumb girls" or your professors, co-workers, and boss won't take you seriously.

I competed in my mid-20's while I was in graduate school working for the Vice President of my University. I had to break it to the whole office that if I won the local title; I'd be out for a full week during the summer for the state pageant. Fortunately, I was prepared for their confusion and had some pretty impressive – and honest – responses, which I'll share with you in the next chapter.

Remember that most of the naysayers are people that simply don't know what a pageant is or don't understand the industry. You know more than they do about pageantry and if you've asked yourself all of these questions, you'll be prepared to prove your argument and they'll be excited to cheer you on!

41: 5 Real-Life Benefits of Pageantry

WinAPageant.com/41

The pageant industry is small and mostly mysterious to outsiders who have never been involved in a pageant. Therefore, you may find yourself explaining your decision to compete over and over again. I'm going to make that much easier on you by identifying the five real-life benefits that you gain from simply competing in a pageant – even if you don't win. Each benefit fits into one of the following areas of life: social, professional, personal, financial, or health. These benefits are ones that are widely recognized by the general population, so they are great tools to explain to your boss why you need two weeks off mid-August to travel to Vegas.

Benefit #1 – Social

The first benefit is social, which is probably the most obvious. Pageant women are rarely at a loss for words, and that's simply because they have an understanding of how to communicate with different types of people properly, no matter what the setting. When you are finished talking to a woman who has competed in pageants, you usually feel really great about yourself because she's been trained to truly show other people their inner beauty. When you compete in pageants, you learn how to experience new people and new settings, proper etiquette, how to have a conversation, and how to show gratitude.

Manners don't come naturally. They have to be learned. I mean, there are many, many times when you may compete in a pageant where you're kind of dumped into a situation you've never been in before. And you need to take your social cues from those around you. That's why one of the benefits of pageantry is learning how to handle a variety of social situations.

Recently, I was at a wedding shower with other women and the host had finally brought out this beautiful, luscious looking cake to cut. There was one woman there who was extremely anxious to try the cake, so much so that instead of minding her manners and keeping her wits about herself, she reached out with her finger and swiped some icing off of the cake and licked her finger! I was absolutely horrified! You would never, ever, ever see a pageant woman do something like that because pageant women are placed in social situations all the time where they are trained to watch their surroundings, follow the lead of the host of any event, and mind their manners. This cake-swiping woman was really nice and fun to be around, she was just never taught proper manners.

Benefit #2 – Professional

The second benefit comes in a woman's professional life. Most pageants include a speaking or interview component. You learn the concepts of interviewing that are transferrable to your profession. Networking is a major component of pageantry and vital to your career. "Your network is your net worth," as they say. Learning how to formulate your pageant paperwork translates to understanding how to put professional documents together so others are able to read them easier. Work ethic is also quickly developed in those that excel in pageantry.

Benefit #3 – Personal

The third benefit, personal development, is likely one of the deepest and most transformative benefits of competing. Things like gaining confidence, interacting with people, understanding how to put together an outfit, styling your hair and makeup, risk tolerance, crisis management, self-value, independence, and overcoming obstacles are all skills for becoming a leader in any industry, community, or organization. The challenges of pageantry help cultivate these personal skills that ultimately make you a better human being.

I started competing in pageants around age 18, and admittedly, I was more independent than most people, but I grew into this more and more. I give credit to my sense of independence, responsibility, and adventure for allowing me to move across the country. I took a cross-country road trip 3,000 miles from Pennsylvania to Los Angeles, where

I knew nobody, not a single soul. I learned how to cultivate relationships, navigate new experiences, and build a life I adore!

Benefit #4 – Financial

The fourth benefit is financial. Participating in pageants is a great opportunity for young girls to start exploring proper money management and budgeting. This skill when learned early will pay off over and over again. Fundraising and cultivating sponsors are valuable skills you'll learn in pageantry and will be able to apply to your future. Knowing the difference between price and value as well as what you're able to offer will be helpful as you negotiate future job opportunities and paid appearances.

Benefit #5 – Physical

The fifth benefit is your physical health. Your physical health flourishes because of your mindfulness of fitness and nutrition to fuel a busy lifestyle in the public eye. Your mental health is challenged and redefined when you overcome difficult situations. Your spiritual health is strengthened when you see the laws of the universe come to play in your pageant year. Universal concepts like "you reap what you sow," "ask and you shall receive," and "thoughts become things" basically become second nature.

Because of the nature of a pageant incorporating so many elements of the human experience into the competition, you have unlimited opportunities for learning – even if you aren't trying. However, if you are trying to grow into your greatest potential, you're in the right place.

70: Calculating the Actual Value of Your Pageant Prize Package

WinAPageant.com/70

You know that there are costs involved in every hobby and career move, and pageants are no different. It's not easy to win a pageant, there is a lot you have to afford, give up, and buckle down on. If you have to refinance your house or postpone your sister's heart surgery just to compete in a pageant, you may want to at least make sure the juice is worth the squeeze.

Some women end up winning pageants and then are shocked to discover the prize package is rather sparse and the title is more trouble than it's worth. You know how the pageant may say the prize package is a whopping $75,000, but it turns out this is mostly in-kind gifts? It happens often. If you only use $500 of the in-kind gifts, it's really only worth $500 to you, right?

I want to show you how to calculate the actual value of your pageant prize package to *you*. This six step Prize Package Calculation process will help you identify how much the pageant is really worth, which will help you to prepare your budget, and help you decide what you'll give up and where you draw the line.

Step #1 – Create a spreadsheet with four columns and several rows. You could do this on your computer or with a pencil and paper, whichever feels good to you.

Step #2 – The first column is where we'll take inventory of what comes with a win. I call it "gifts and obligations." Write down each thing you receive and each thing you are obligated to do down the first column – one item in each row. For example, if you are getting a crown and sash, bouquet of flowers, a photography session with a local photographer, a pair of ice skates, and a $500,000 scholarship to a chiropractic school, put each one of these in a row in the first column. An obligation would be attending a certain event as an official appearance, competing at the

National pageant, or doing a photo shoot with a famed photographer. Write down all the things you're aware of – most of it you'll be looking forward to, even the obligations.

Step #3 – In the second column, we're going to record the Opportunity Value. Go through each of the gifts and obligations you wrote and consider the value each will bring to your life over the next two years. Write these in the second column in the same row as the gift or obligation. For example, maybe attending the mandatory Macy's Thanksgiving Day Parade will allow you to experience a famous event like you never have before or introduce you to the right people for your future career. To discover the value you'll really be receiving, consider how you'll grow and develop, whom you'll meet, and what you'll get to do.

Step #4 – In the third column, you'll write the Opportunity Cost over two years: What will you have to give up? This column is the shadow side to the gifts and obligations. Write down what you'll have to give up to accomplish this thing or enjoy this gift. If you have to miss your annual family vacation to go to the National, write that here. Nothing is too small or too large. We'll assign numerical value in the next step.

Step #5 – Consider how much each gift and obligation costs. You'll have to assign a monetary/numerical value to each opportunity value and cost. Pay special attention to the things that have monetary value, but are of no use to you. If it's worthless, give it a $0 even if someone else would pay a million dollars for it. If the opportunity is your time or personal development, assign a number next to it that it's worth to you. If you don't really care to miss your family vacation to the beach because you see your cousins every weekend anyway, then it may be a lower number. If you haven't seen your family from Italy for a decade and they won't be back again, then it may be a higher number. This step is really personal, so if there is something you absolutely wouldn't give up, it's okay to put $1billion on it.

Step #6 – Now, let's get a concrete number difference. Add up all of the numbers in column 3 (this is the positive value). Subtract the total from column 4 (the cost) and you'll be left with either a positive or negative number.

The point of this exercise is less about the final number that you reach. It's more about exploring the feeling you have when you see the results. If it's heavily swayed to the positive and you still have a yucky feeling, you'll have to consider why before entering the pageant. If the results are negative, but you go back through your list and figure out a way to make it work, then you'll be realize nothing is holding you back and it will propel you and motivate your efforts.

Whatever you do, don't be fooled – not all pageants bring value. Usually "you get out of it, what you put into it." But if this pageant is asking you to give up more than it's worth, it's okay to walk away before you sign the dotted line. Be clear on the vision and how it applies to your own life. Don't let someone else's dream become your reality.

43: The 3 Reasons Women Lose Pageants

WinAPageant.com/43

After every pageant, the women that don't win have similar reactions, excuses, and reasons for why they weren't really suited to win. Their insights can provide a lot of understanding and teach you to avoid these common pitfalls.

Losing Reason #1 – Unrealistic Expectations
When you first saw someone ice skating it was likely someone that knew what she was doing. Maybe you watched Disney on Ice or went to your babysitter's skating recital. When someone is excellent at something, they make it look easy. Pageantry is no different. When you watch a woman waltz onto stage and gracefully glide around and float off, you too may actually think it's easy. It's not. But that doesn't stop women from joining a pageant and then being shocked by all the work that goes into it.

People also underestimate the caliber of women that compete. There is a stereotype that pageant women aren't smart or lack substance. The truth is that these women are generally playing at the top of their game. They are super smart, resourceful, successful and driven. Everyone has the qualities they need to succeed, but women who don't win think they don't need to discover and nurture their strengths. This leads them to ignore the need for development and attempt to rely on what's gotten them to where they are now. That's backward thinking. If you want to go beyond where you've always gone, you need skills beyond what you've always had.

After a pageant, the women that have lost often reflect on the fact that they simply didn't know how to prepare – they misunderstand the process. These women don't realize that there is a system to preparation. There is timing to how things are gathered, implemented, executed, prepared, and performed. The seed that you're planting today is what you'll harvest tomorrow.

Losing Reason #2 – Resistance to Invest

In many cases, women lose pageants because they are resistant to invest in their dream. Maybe they believe that pageantry is only judging what you have now. If that were the case, then they'd just pull 50 women from the street, look in their closets, ask them to sing, and put a crown on one. Pageantry isn't about judging what you can do with what you have. It's judging what you can do with who you are.

Some women don't want to invest in their wardrobe, their training, or their self-care. The truth is that pageantry really does demand investment. What you lack in finances you need to make up in time. What you lack in time you need to make up in finances. I have a mentor who's told me that everyone wants things that are fast, cheap, and good, but you can only have two at a time. You can have fast and cheap, but it won't be good. You can have good and cheap, but it won't be fast. You can have fast and good, but it won't be cheap. When you approach your pageant with an abundance of time and finances, your experience will likely be good because you'll be able to afford it with time and finances.

When I started competing, I didn't have extra finances to spend, but I was willing to put in a lot of time. I chose to compete in the pageants that had high scholarship dollars and a lot of support. When I won, I used the earnings and support to learn everything I could and prepare me for the next year. It was good and it was cheap, but it wasn't fast. When I was in my final year of competition before aging out, I finally hired a coach because I needed my training to be fast – it was my final year, and I didn't have time to waste. It was fast and it was good, but it wasn't cheap. Fortunately, I'd been saving and was smart about sponsorships by then from the ten years I'd be learning, so I was more prepared than ever and it paid off with a win!

Investing isn't the same as spending. Spending is generally unwise. Someone who spends usually doesn't follow a budget, has little vision, and ends up not putting in the energy to make the cost of time or money wise. An example of this is someone sitting at their computer for hours and days flipping through various YouTube makeup tutorials trying to learn how to apply their own makeup. Without a time budget, an ultimate vision of stage makeup, and valuing the process, she wastes tons of time and end up no better off than when she sat down to begin with. Another example is the woman that buys dresses like she's going to the prom every weekend. Instead of carrying a vision for her brand and a budget for her wallet, she ends up over spending on something that may not be ideal for her.

Dumping money and time into things leads to success. To be successful in pageantry, you'll have to invest. Investing is getting educated on what's needed then carefully crafting a budget of resources until the goal is met. Investing requires a give before a get. When you pay for a product you're making a financial energy exchange. You give money for someone's energy and knowledge. When you hire a personal trainer, you pay them money in exchange for them to train you how to get to your goals. I give free pageant trainings every week on the Win A Pageant iTunes podcast (WinAPageant.com/iTunes). As a result, I receive a lot of thank you notes and beautiful gifts in the mail when women win their pageants. I'm investing in their success and the best ones recognize it as an energy exchange, so they honor it by giving back with gratitude, reviews, and recommendations.

Losing Reason #3 – Imposter Syndrome

The most common reason women do not win is because of what we call the impostor syndrome. This is when you feel like you're pretending to be someone you're not. When we are doing something we've never done before, we sometimes carry a negative mindset that we don't deserve to be doing this new thing. It's a fear-based thought that leads us to doubt ourselves, doubt our calling, and doubt our ability. Of course, if you'd done it before, you'd be certain you could do it. But there's a first time for everything.

To avoid these three pitfalls, gather knowledge to understand what to expect of the industry and the pageant you're participating in. Be willing to invest your resources to become your best self. Trust that if you've prepared properly, you'll have what it takes to be a huge success.

CHAPTER 2

CULTIVATE A WINNING MINDSET

4: To Win or Not to Win: Determine Your Ultimate Goal

WinAPageant.com/4

To win or not to win, that is the question. Just because you enter a pageant, doesn't mean you have to want to win…yes, seriously. Pageant contestants sometimes get caught up in the need to win without truly considering what they really want. In this lesson, I'll teach you a 4-step exercise to help you determine your ultimate goal. This exercise is also helpful for every pageant you enter because it can bring out some hidden fears that you weren't even aware of. These fears and insecurities can keep you from winning the title – unless you surface them now.

Step #1 – Write a list of all the reasons you do want to win (try to write at least 10)

Step #2 – Write a list of all the reasons you don't want to win (try to write at least 10)

Step #3 – Examine the "Don't" list and for every idea you wrote down, label it either rational (meaning, it's real and has a real impact) or irrational (meaning it's silly and you can get over it).

Step #4 – For the irrational ones, create a counterargument to nix that from the Don't List. For example, if you wrote that you don't want to win because you're afraid you'll break out by wearing makeup, you can nix that by saying you'll find the best makeup for your face and practice good skin care so that you don't break out. There. Problem solved. For the rational ideas – the ones that are worth taking seriously – ask yourself if this is something that you can live with as a titleholder or if this is worth not winning the pageant over. For example, if you have to give up your Harvard law school acceptance or postpone your own wedding, these may be reasons to not win.

The true development comes in doing this exercise. It's different for everyone, and as you start digging, things will come up that may surprise you. Once you've gone through this exercise, you'll have a better idea of what is truly holding you back from winning. If there is nothing noteworthy, then you can put all your eggs in the Winner basket and go for the gold!!

On the website for this specific lesson, you can see the list I made when I was competing in the International pageant system. It's a good example of this exercise applied to real life. Take a look at: WinAPageant.com/4

39: Pageant Goal Setting to Make This "Your Year"

WinAPageant.com/39

Several years ago, a mentor of mine named Scot explained the concept of The Year of Scot. "The Year of You" involves focusing on what makes you happy, becoming a better version of yourself, accomplishing your vision, and having a wildly successful year full of what makes you uniquely you. That was about 5 years ago, and since then, every year has been The Year of Alycia.

With the motivation to celebrate my year (every year), I studied Spanish in Costa Rica and Argentina, moved across the country, attended events like Tony Robbins's Unleash the Power Within and Life on Fire's Ignite, got certified in many fitness techniques, changed careers (twice), became a model, spokesperson, and TV host, started a business, a podcast, a blog, a YouTube channel, and met my husband. I have accomplished so much in the last 5 years as a result of this goal-setting motivation I call "Your Year."

The beauty of dedicating the full year to you are that it becomes less about the outcome of a particular situation and more focused on the growth during the journey. Instead of being concerned with what you can't control, you shift your focus to what you can control. Of course, it's not about being selfish; it's about prioritizing your activities to support your dreams.

Women have differing reasons for wanting to win a pageant. Lots of women want to win to further a particular cause, experience the limelight of celebrity, and be rushed off into fun and interesting experiences, or hob-nob with the debutants. Whatever your reason, I promise you, it's not the crown that makes you achieve it, but rather all the work that prepares you for the crown. This is one of the biggest misconceptions: that you have to win to achieve success. The truth is the winners are already achieving success, that's why they win.

There are many types of goals. The most common is outcome goals, which are typically measured with numbers, dollars, and percentages. This includes key performance indicators like the average number of appearances you make in a month, the increased dollar amount of donations at your fundraiser, the lowered percent of people at-risk. Those outcome goals are directly tied to a series of actions that you have control over.

The other form of goal setting, which we'll unpack here, is Process Goals: things that are learned, accomplished, or developed during the journey toward the outcome goal.

Follow these three steps to set your own process goals:

Step #1 – Brainstorm the things that are most important for you to gain from the year. What do you want to learn? What skills do you want to develop? How do you want to stretch yourself to grow? Who will your Legacy Project reach this year? What new adventures do you want to have? Dream on and on – keep thinking of things until you have a list of about 25 things or more.

Step #2 – Read through your list again. Ask yourself which ones aren't really that important to you. Cross them out. No sense cluttering your brain with ideas that don't really matter. You'll likely have about 10-15 process goals. Don't settle for the first 10 that come to mind, though. Usually those are the ones that get thrown out because they came off the top of your head rather than being created from your deeper creative power.

Step #3 – Read your list again. Ask yourself which ones are relying on something you can't control. For these ones, either re-write them to focus on the process or just scratch them off your life. For example, if you wrote that you want to convince Google to donate $20,000 to your platform, re-write it to say, "Learn the best way to gain high-level sponsors that could donate $20,000 for my platform."

Usually process goals take longer than a few weeks to accomplish. It can take closer to a full month or sometimes a year. Plus, you have to remember that YOU are responsible for accomplishing these during your process. All of these goals are growth-oriented and will pay off in real life beyond pageantry. When you are focused on learning to choose clothes that flatter your figure and personality, you'll make much better choices with pageant wardrobe when the time comes. Do you see how this works for women that are in pageantry for the long haul? Year after year, they are learning new skills that apply to pageants and to real life – that is why they are successful. That is why I only work with clients that have a big vision, a 5-year plan. We don't compete to just win the pageant; we compete to win in life. Some of my clients' goals include things like learning how to network at a cocktail party, learning to read a teleprompter, successfully hosting a live event, or knowing how to choose clothes that work best for them while shopping.

Your goals are a part of the process, and they will take time. But by this time next year, you will have achieved so much. Make this your year, girl!

56: Winners Take Action: The 3 Steps to Achieve Your Big Goal

WinAPageant.com/56

I want to share with you a key to success. It's simple, but it is not easy. It's called action. Taking action is the number one thing that separates the good from the excellent – all the people with amazing ideas from those with amazing results. Taking action means using the knowledge that you're gaining from teachers, coaches, podcasts, experiences, and even this book, and allowing it to flow through your strengths and your skills and take action to help others.

People who don't take action aren't releasing their knowledge into the world. Imagine a running creek of water that is constantly refreshed, taking in new information and sharing it on down the road. If nothing is flowing through you, you're either a swampland or a flood. If you aren't gaining anything new to pass along, you're swampy. If you are only gaining new information and not taking action to let it flow through you, you're flooding. Other people can tell if you're swampy or flooding and no one wants to work with someone that is seen as swampy or flooding – not even pageant judges.

To be successful in pageants and in your life, you need to take action to make an impact.

There are three simple steps to taking action:

Step #1 – Decide which one thing you can implement within the next 24 hours. Make it small and manageable.

Step #2 – Write down in your calendar when you will find the time to accomplish this.

Step #3 – When the time comes, do the thing you said you'd do.

I have a sad story of a client that is not an action-taker. A client that I worked with last year that has an incredible story and a brilliant idea for a book. I met with her for an hour. She competed a few months later and hadn't made progress on her book, but that's okay because it was only a few months between creating the idea and competing in her pageant. She didn't win, which I'm not surprised because she didn't really go all in. That's not even the sad part. The sad part is, she competed again in the same pageant, an entire year later — and she still hasn't taken action on her book idea. She was asked about her book (again) in her on stage question and had to announce that it was still only an idea and it hadn't been written yet. Did she win? Nope.

Everyone has ideas. Only the successful people put them into action.

Emaleigh is 18, she's in honors courses, she's the president of three school organizations, she just got into Penn State University, and she's a varsity team captain. This girl has the world by the tail. She's an action-taker like none other. We've been working together for a few months now and she is only two months away from publishing her first book. She's starting college in her freshman year as a published author! How cool is that?

A Mrs. contestant, Candice, join my VIP jump-start program two months before her pageant. In two months she created a YouTube channel and brought on two sponsors to help her fund her Legacy Project. After she won her national title, she said her entire interview was easy because it was about her Legacy Project. They were so impressed by her success and vision; they couldn't stop talking about it.

Taking action is vital to success in pageantry and in life. I want this to be a part of your everyday life. What goal do you want to achieve? What is something you can do within the next 24 hours to make progress toward your goal? Look at your calendar and plug that one thing into your calendar immediately.

62: What's Your Pageant Vision? (Defining Success in Pageantry)

WinAPageant.com/62

"Where there is no vision, the people will perish, but happy are the people that keep the law." ~ Proverbs 29:18

Vision is what drives action. Without vision the actions are all over the place, running to the left and right instead of staying the course toward the end goal, the ultimate vision. Of all areas of competition, it seems women are most nervous about interview. Yet, every now and then you'll meet a woman who lives for the interview! The difference begins with vision.

When you have a vision, you can inspire people around you to join your movement and follow the path with you. Without vision, you perish. You get all caught up in what you aren't doing and comparison to the vision of others, you don't have a path to walk down and you're basically lost in the sauce.

Every successful pageant woman has a vision. You need one too! Let's break down the steps that you'll take to create your vision.

Step #1 – We are a product of the 10 people we spend the most time with. The same is true for every area of your life – you are what you eat, what you consume, what you read, what you say, how you think, how you behave. Start by taking inventory of what is currently influencing you. Do not judge yourself in this exercise. This is strictly about awareness. We can change these things moving forward, but we have to first know what they are. Just be honest. Write a list of the top 10 people (boss, colleagues, boyfriend, mom, three sorority sisters, roommate, husband, you get the idea), top 10 sources of information (audio books, radio, TV show you binge watch, your gossipy girlfriend, your pastor, mentor, podcasts you listen to, books you read, newspaper, magazines), top 10 images you see (laptop background image, view from your desk, classroom, library, office, living room, kitchen – what is in your environment?), top 10 smells (body odor of your cubicle-mate, day-old garbage, candles, strawberries, fresh cut grass), top 10 moves you make, your habits (like slouching, yoga, flipping your hair, high fiving your partner, kissing your husband, typing at a computer, answering the phone, reading), and top 10 phrases or words you say (totally, so good, I know, yup, she is so, I can't even, I love you).

Step #2 – Now, in step two, we judge. Everything in our environment holds a positive or negative impact on us by association. Some people call this "positive energy or vibrations." You can feel it the most with music. Turn on a song with Eminem screaming nasty things at you over an angry beat and you'll want to punch a wall. Turn on a happy beat and positive lyrics and you'll want to clap along and smile at everyone you pass by. Am I right? Well, guess what? Your judges can feel this too. When they are meeting so many women with great looks and skills, the thing that stands out most is their energy. Look at your list. Next to everything you wrote down put a plus sign next to the things that add positivity, abundance, happiness, joy, and love to your life. Next to everything and everyone that weighs you down, tears you up, adds problems, or sucks your energy, draw a line through it. Usually, the areas of your life with the most plus signs are the areas of life that we thrive in. These areas are what we want to share and talk about and the areas that you've crossed out are the ones you want to escape.

Step #3 – In the third step you'll create your vision of total health, wellness, happiness, joy, and all over awesomeness so you are prepared to step into the role of the rightful pageant winner! Get a new piece of paper and write the top 10 things you WANT in your life in each category you completed before: people, sources of information, images, smells, moves, and words/phrases. You will likely want to surround yourself with uplifting and successful pageant women, maybe a positive pageant coach, supportive friends. You may want to gather information from credible sources, get book recommendations for uplifting and informative reading. Maybe you want a beautiful new apartment, or a closet full of the latest fashions and fancy pageant gowns. You may love the smell of the hairspray your favorite salon uses when you pay $40 for a blowout, or the smell of fresh squeezed orange juice. Maybe you want to walk in heels more or know how to dance for opening number. Maybe you want to practice walking, waving, or just standing with confidence. Maybe you want to shift your language to build people up and be a joy to be around. This is the kind of stuff I want you thinking about. How can you become the woman you know you are meant to be to win this pageant!

Step #4 – Once you know the keys that make up your vision in your mind, put it into your environment. We need to train your mind to see other things that will shift your brain and body into a new direction. That is the power of a Vision Board. A vision board is basically a collage of images that build your life in the direction you want it to move. It includes only positive and uplifting images that symbolize information, people, smells, foods, moves, and words that we want to surround ourselves with. To take this one step further, start doing the things you need to get you closer to your vision: drive around the ritziest neighborhood near you, listen to the music of your favorite artist, take a bubble bath, make a dish that has all the flavors that delight you, dust off your favorite book, call your old friend. Get these beautiful things back into your realm.

Step #5 – When your vision board is in front of you, you are far more likely to take action towards this effort. You'll become (not just want to become) the woman you desire to be, the woman you know is positioned to win. That is your goal and the reason that successful women have a vision of success.

Without a vision, the people perish. With a vision, the sky's the limit!

35: The Comprehensive Pageant Preparation Plan

WinAPageant.com/35

There are four phases of the Comprehensive Pageant Preparation Plan that I guide my VIP clients through: foundation, communication, representation, and implementation. These phases are broken into 10 steps. The length of time spent in each phase varies. For a printable list of these phases to map out your pageant timeline, download the Beauty, Truth and Grace Guidebook at: WinAPageant.com/Guide.

Let's go through each phase and step so you can know where to begin your preparation.

Phase 1: Foundation

Step #1 – The first step that I walk each of my clients through is understanding herself. What are your strengths, what are your desires, and what do you value? When you understand this as a foundational background, you're not going to get hung up on interview questions, an on-stage question, your paperwork, or anything else. This is because you're going to truly know each of these things about you.

One of my biggest frustrations is when a woman is asked to name three things that are great about herself and she struggles. You should not struggle – you really ought to know what your strengths are, you need to know what you want, and you need to know the value you bring to the table.

Step #2 – The next step is to define your purpose. What is your legacy and what is the greater impact that you want to have on the world?

Step #3 – The third step of phase one is determining your goal. When you decide your legacy and your impact, you need to give it a concrete goal. We usually talk about numbers, dollars, and percentages. That is what constitutes your purpose. In this step, take a look at your platform. Yes, even Miss USA contestants must have a platform. A platform gives you added value because you've got something to stand on. Also, consider your partnerships and network.

My training programs always include these Foundational elements because I believe success is vital to understanding who you are, your purpose, and your goals. Phase two is where you learn how to communicate all those awesome things about who you are, your purpose, and your goals.

Phase 2: Communication.

Step #4 – Step four falls into this phase and that is your paperwork. The first thing the judges see that will communicate your foundation is your paperwork. Communication is, indeed, partially the way in which you talk and how you understand yourself, but it's mostly the way in which others understand and perceive you. Being able to communicate your values, strengths, and purpose is important.

Step #5 – The fifth step, also related to communication, is public speaking. Interviewing and on-stage questions are both examples of public speaking and important parts of pageantry.

Step #6 – The sixth step is your presence. Believe it or not, your presence is also a method of communication. Your presence is your body language, how you carry yourself during on-stage modeling and at events. You must communicate your strengths, values, purpose, and goals with your presence.

Phase 3: Representation
    This phase is made up of steps six, seven, and eight.

Steps #6, #7, and #8 – These include wardrobe, photographs and marketing. The way in which you brand yourself with your chosen wardrobe shows other people what you represent. Photographs should be authentically you and reflect your true personality. The judges do not want to look at a photograph and then the woman who walks in looks completely different. You want to have a photographer that captures your essence. You've got to be prepared to show up for that photographer so that any photographer should be able to take your images and they will look authentically like you.

Step #9 – Step nine in the representation phase is marketing. A lot of pageant women like to believe the lie that they do not need to market themselves or that the pageant will do all the marketing for them. Believe it or not, social media promotion, how many tickets you sell, the network that you have and what events you attend are all a part of marketing you. These are vital to your pageant preparation and, of course, your pageant success.

Phase 4: Implementation

This is the phase that consumes the least amount of time and energy when all the other phases are managed properly.

Step #10 – This includes your pageant week mindset. It also includes you taking responsibility for leading your team of makeup artist, hair stylist, sponsors, audience members, and even your fellow contestants and directors during pageant week. Your leadership as a pageant titleholder is vital. In this area of implementation, you have to remain consistent across all stages of competition, from sun up to sun down, whether you're on stage or off stage.

Having an understanding of this comprehensive pageant preparation plan will help you remember that winning takes effort. You'll honor the women that have worked hard to accomplish their dreams, and you'll train to be the very best. The winners that are the absolute best have been trained by the best, and they've put so much time and effort into it that it actually looks easy.

You can get the printable 10-step Pageant Preparation Plan inside the Beauty, Truth and Grace Guidebook. Download it for free at: WinAPageant.com/Guide.

8: Visualizing Your Win

WinAPageant.com/8

Visualizing your win is a powerful exercise to believe (subconsciously) that you are suited to win the pageant. If you can watch yourself winning, you are far more likely to deeply believe that you'll actually take the crown.

I've written a guided meditation that will help you to visualize yourself winning your pageant. You can listen to the guided visualization at WinAPageant.com/8.

Of course, my guided path won't be as specific as you could be. What would be more powerful is for you to create your own mind movie of everything from orientation to giving your acceptance speech at the new titleholder. The idea here is to close your eyes, be completely relaxed and really feel all the emotions that come up for you during this experience. Get cozy into a chair, maybe lying down, and go ahead and close your eyes and use your mind's eye to guide you through this exercise. I want you to start by just taking a deep breath in.

Imagine yourself backstage. Imagine how the lights will feel and your excitement as you stand backstage before opening number. Visualize yourself walking across stage – feel it in your body and watch as your eyes make eye contact with the judges in the first row. Imagine yourself gracefully executing each phase of competition. Imagine your name being called for the top ten, then the top five. Imagine yourself standing next to one other woman as the host announces her as the first runner-up and you as the winning of the pageant! How will you feel? How will you look? Who will be there with you? If you know what to see in advance, you won't be shocked that it's happening in real life.

If your goal is to win, you have to know what to expect. Practice helps, so practice with this visualization. Do this visualization several times, if not daily, leading up to your pageant, especially during your pageant week. The week leading up to your pageant and the night before your pageant, are going to be key times. As you're preparing and the closer you get, the more clear your actual winning moment will become to you.

CHAPTER 3

UNDERSTAND YOUR JUDGES

76: 5 Real Reasons Judges Judge Pageants

WinAPageant.com/76

When I was competing, long before I ever judged a pageant, I always felt like the judges were out to get me. Like I was a freshman on my first day in high school and they were the nasty seniors trying to trip me in the hallway. Isn't that an awful mental image? Do you ever feel that way? It was so real to me at that time!

And then I judged my first pageant and my perspective totally changed. I've since judged many pageants – everything from Little Miss Lakeville to Miss California.

As a judge, you get to hang out with the directors behind the scenes, you see what every girl brings to the table, you get to ask the questions you want to know about, you get to go out to dinner with the other judges and chit-chat about life, and then you get to be a part of changing a woman's entire life – all in one weekend! It's pretty incredible!

The experience of judging helped me see that the judges are really FOR you (the contestant), not against you. Instead of the nasty senior trying to trip you, they're really more like the senior math tutor that meets you after school and helps you study. When you get an A, they text you an adorable A+ Bitmoji. Seriously! That's your judge!

I want to break down for you 5 real reasons that judges want to be on a judging panel. I hope this gives you the insight you need to relax and do your part to showcase your best self for them.

Reason #1 – The most common reason that judges end up judging a pageant is to help out their friend who is the director of the pageant. This is usually the case for when someone is asked to judge his or her first pageant. They want to volunteer their time to assist with something that is clearly so important to their friend (your pageant director) and have heard such beautiful things over the years so they want to help and are happy to be involved.

Reason #2 – Another common reason is they want to be a part of all the hubbub! They know that pageants are a big deal. There's a certain level of mystery to what really goes on behind the curtain, so they want to see what it's all about and check "judge a pageant" off their bucket list.

Reason #3 – Some pageant judges want to be the one that selects the winner. They want to say, "I chose Miss Florida." I'm sure you hear people every year after Miss America say something like, "Yeah, I had her picked from her introduction." People love this! It's like hand-selecting the star of everyone's favorite TV show and then saying, "Yeah, you have me to thank."

Reason #4 – Sometimes judges feel like they want to uncover a diamond in the rough. They are rooting for the underdog and want to watch a woman rise with confidence and empowerment under the intense pressure of a pageant. They want to see a rags-to-riches story unfold and they want their part in it. These judges have a heart for the least likely candidates and have a special gift of dusting off the dirt to uncover your gold.

Reason #5 – Most judges want to judge a pageant because they want to draw the winning lottery ticket for someone that makes their dreams come true! Imagine if you had the power to pull the Million Dollar Lotto and then you got to immediately usher that person onto a stage and take photos with them on the day of their win. How exciting would that be? You'd have an instant connection with this new celebrity and you'd have a hand in making their dreams come true!

I've learned so much from judging on a variety of panels – not just about the process that goes into scoring, calibrating, calculating, and delivering results, but also in the passion and motivation of each judge in the room. They aren't there to trip you up. They aren't trying to be nasty. They aren't out to hurt you. They are hoping for a diamond, looking for a gem, searching for the gold in everyone and they want their work to make your dreams to true. Your job is to dazzle them by spoon-feeding them exactly what they need to see to reveal your gold and root for you.

96: 7 Things Judges Think about Your Old Titles on Your Pageant Paperwork

WinAPageant.com/96

I believe the top 10 contestants can usually be selected from paperwork alone. Most pageant women don't put a lot of thought or effort into their paperwork. They write some nice answers and move on without considering how these answers will affect their perception even before they arrive for the interview. For my clients we take days crafting paperwork to guide the interview and give them a leg up. One question that comes up a lot is whether or not they should put their old pageant title on another pageant's paperwork.

For example, if they were Miss Great Lakes 2014 in the Miss America Organization, they wonder if they should put that on their application for the Miss USA Pageant.

People have differing opinions on this and because each system is so different, there's not really a right or wrong way. Instead, I will share with you seven thoughts a judge may have when they see (or don't see) past titles on your paperwork. Hopefully this gives you the insight you need to help you decide for yourself.

When a judge sees a past title on the paperwork they may think:

Thought #1 – "Oh, goodie! This one's gonna be good!" If that is totally true and you are head and shoulders above your competition, then do it! If you truly know you aren't an outlier, then leave it off. You'll get scored lower if you don't live up to their inflated expectations.

Thought #2 – "Oh, good. She knows what to expect with a title." If your past title and the title you're competing for is more of a lateral move or a down-step in terms of audience reach and level of responsibility, then keep it on there. For example, if you were Miss USA and you're competing for Miss World, I say leave it on there. If you were Miss Glory of the Heartlands and now you're competing for

Miss Three Rivers, then keep it on there. However, don't put Miss Glory of the Heartlands 2013 on your 2016 application for Miss New York.

Thought #3 – "Oh, boy. We have a lifer." This could put an instant target on your head. Especially if you list out like five former titles over the last seven years, you may get an eye roll and someone looking to trip you off of your "Pageant Patty" persona in search for someone that isn't just chasing a crown. In this case, if you put it on there, you'll want to make sure you come off incredibly warm, friendly, and normal.

Thought #4 – "Cool, I'm excited to talk to this one." If your judge loves pageant women, she's going to love you. She'll feel connected like she has something to talk about and trust that you know what you're doing. If you don't impress her, she may be disappointed and could score you extra low to give someone else the opportunity.

Thought #5 – "Uh-oh. This girl may not be loyal." Some pageant systems prefer you only speak of their pageant. It makes sense – if you were representing Pepsi, they wouldn't want you talking about how you had a great year when you worked for Coke. You'll have to be prepared to express why you're overly interested in this new system. It will have to be better than, "well, I aged out of the other one, so thought I'd try it here." Be prepared.

When a judge sees no past titles on the paperwork they may think:
Thought #6 – "Hmm…I wonder if she has experience." Sometimes the judges really do want you to have pageant experience. Some pageant directors actually ask the judges to greatly consider contestants with prior experience, especially in their system because it usually makes for a better year. For these pageants, you'll want to show up looking like a total pro and maybe even bring up your experience in your interview if you don't put it on there.

Thought #7 – Or they may think nothing at all. They may not even notice and they'll lump you in with all the other girls that didn't put titles on their paperwork. You'll come in with a fresh slate and they may still ask you (especially if you show up well prepared and obviously experienced), but then you're a pleasant surprise.

The bottom line is this: It's usually safe to include your past title if you are making a lateral move (one national pageant to another) or if you're competing at the higher level within your pageant system (from state to national). The most important thing to consider is how you'll walk into the first round of competition. If you say you have experience, you better show up prepared, sharp, engaging, and talented. They'll be expecting a winner and you'll have to be ready to prove yourself. If you are, then I say go for it! Put it on there loud and proud, and prepare yourself to prove your awesomeness.

71: Choosing Your Contestant Number

WinAPageant.com/71

It doesn't take long after your first pageant until you start to question the validity that all contestant numbers are equal. In pageant land, it's long been thought that being contestant number one is sure death. There is some truth to that argument, but there are three additional opinions about the argument of "which contestant number should I choose" if given the option.

Some pageants assign contestant numbers, others draw from a hat, and still others draw from a hat for the women to choose their own number. No matter what, it will be useful for you to understand how your contestant number may affect your judging.

Here are the three opinions to the contestant number decision and how you can apply each to help you choose your contestant number.

Opinion #1 – Set the Bar – leading the pageant as contestant number one is no easy task. You are the first to break the ice and set the bar for the rest of the contestants. If you are in the beginning half of the competition, you absolutely must set precedence beyond the others. This works well for the girl that is super strong in the first area of competition – I'm talking, head and shoulders above the competition. If you made it to the finals in season six of "So You Think You Can Dance," and your competition opens with talent, you need to choose contestant number one. You will set the bar so high that everything else will be a disappointment. If, however, you are doing a flute diddle-dum-dee that you just learned in the last three months, then you should avoid being placed in the first half of the lineup.

Opinion #2 – Start Low – the next side of the story, which is why most people avoid the first half of the lineup, is the idea that judges tend to give low numbers at the beginning with hopes of leaving space to be wowed by a surprise 10. If you are a mediocre contender (which you never should be; you should always be the stand-out winner, but it does happen that we compete for different reasons) then being in the first half of the lineup is absolute death by low scoring. You will get unfairly low scores and be remembered as not being the wowzer in the middle, so you'll continue to get lower scores. If, however you are average at most areas of competition, but the first area of competition is your strongest, then being contestant number one isn't so bad after all. If you nail your interview and there are few that can impress beyond you, you'll be the favored one going into the on-stage competition, which will eliminate the compulsion for low scoring.

Opinion #3 – Leave an Impression – the other argument is the idea that you want to be last in the line-up in order to leave a lasting impression. For someone who competes similarly to others or doesn't have a "stand-out" phase of competition, this is a fine place to be, but to be the final contestant is not ideal. You'll fade into the sunset of tallying scores and rushing to catch up from the judge's bench. However, this is excellent placement for someone who is very different from the other contestants. If everyone has a Sherri Hill high-low spangled fun fashion dress and you strut out in a salsa costume, you will be the most exciting part of the show and highly anticipated. Of course, if you walk out in a pigeon costume, you will be anticipated, but not in a positive, high-scoring way. That's a risk you have to be willing to take.

These little things that happen at the judge's table are not things you can control. Often, they aren't even things the judges can easily control. Some pageants tell the judges to not compare and just focus on the individual, but that's tough to do in reality. Plus, some judges are rooting for the underdog and just looking for reasons to give more points to the girl that falls and recovers or the one that grew up on a pig farm. Others have it set in their mind what they believe a queen is and anyone that challenges that doesn't fit into their box and ends up with lower points. You never know what will happen on the day of your pageant and how your contestant number will affect your scores and personal presentation.

It has to be said that if you are the strongest, most standout, hands down winner in every phase of competition, then it doesn't matter where you are in the lineup. If you open the show, you'll get some low scores the first round and the next round they'll score you fairly. If you are in the middle you'll be anticipated and not easily forgotten. If you're in the end, you'll be a wowzer showstopper, and you'll have a 10 before the ink dries on the last girl's 7.

17: Meeting a Judge in an Elevator

WinAPageant.com/17

Many pageants go through leaps and bounds to keep their judges mysterious, even quarantined, when not doing official pageant business. But, as most pageants know, it's a lot of work to keep a group of five adults on a leash for a week.

At any event, conference, concert, or pageant, it's highly likely you could meet some amazing people in the elevator. There may be separate meeting rooms, green rooms, entrance doors, numbered tables and other hierarchical structures set up to separate the VIPs from the wannabes, but the hotel elevator is accessible to everyone.

That's why it's not unusual to meet a judge in an elevator. In fact, it's an amazing opportunity to connect with anyone in a short yet focused amount of time. Think about it: an elevator conversation with a stranger usually only lasts about two minutes and it makes an otherwise awkward moment into a remarkably pleasant one. What else do you do in an elevator but stare at the numbers lighting up above the door in anticipation of your floor? But if you're not prepared for a conversation, those could be the longest two minutes of silence all weekend.

The first time this happened to me, I was about 12 years old. I was at the Tremaine Dance Convention and met one of the cutest master dance teachers in the elevator; he might as well have been Brad Pitt. My teenage friend and I were so caught off guard all we did was freeze, except for a few awkward giggles. When he got off at the next stop, we busted out in screams and squeals asking one another, "Why didn't you say anything?" We were both so shocked that it even happened. Later that same weekend, we ended up on the elevator with another favorite master teacher and major role model (this time a woman), Desiree. This time, I was prepared. When we got onto her elevator, I immediately introduced myself and thanked her for her awesome teaching and choreography. I remember it to be rather well put together, though I'm sure it was mostly gushing about how I adored her. Either way, it was a huge improvement from nothing at all.

In my life and travels, I've had the pleasure of meeting many intriguing people, CEOs, honeymooners, people from my hometown 3,000 miles away, even the fitness icon Mr. Lou Ferrigno, the co-star of the 1970's Pumping Iron and the original Hulk.

This, of course, happens all the time at pageants – a contestant sneaks down to the lobby for a cup of coffee and an apple, hair in rollers and only one eyelash on when she bumps into a judge going up to the 30th floor with her. It's obvious she's a contestant, yet the judge doesn't want to make her feel uncomfortable. It's up to the contestant to say hello.

The elevator introduction is an amazing opportunity to communicate your true, authentic self, consistent with who you are on stage, in the interview room, and in real life. If you've ever met a professional Miss before like Miss USA, Miss America, or Miss International, you'd expect the same from each of them in the elevator – a sweet hello at the very least. Therefore, I expect the same from you. It's so refreshing to meet a woman who has a personality congruent with her performance, wouldn't you agree?

In order to not be caught off guard, you should always be prepared to make a good impression. Beauty is being engaging and making others feel good, so be prepared to be honest, ask good questions, and give fulfilling answers.

The goal is to give the person you're meeting something meaty to engage with. You could say something simple like "Hi, I'm Kara" or "I'm just here for the snacks," but that may not invite conversation, where you can leave them with a great impression of you. Instead, shine a little of your sparkle and make them feel great, too. When you reveal your true self, you give others permission to do the same.

Before any major event, whether it's a pageant, a career fair, or a professional conference – anything where you'll have the chance to meet some cool people (which, let's be honest, could be just about anywhere), consider what type of people you may encounter and how you want to be remembered.

I have a simple outline to help you prepare. I call it Past-Present-Future. Tell them something quick about your past, your present, and your future, and then ask an engaging open-ended question.

I've broken this conversation example into 4 C's to help you to know what to include in your elevator introduction. I've given examples for each element below so you can use it as a framework to create your own.

The Context

"Hi there, I'm Kate. I'm from Orange County. I'm one of the contestants in the Miss category. I can't wait to perform talent tonight! What brings you here?"

"Hi, I'm Stephanie. I'm from Miami. This curly hair is so grateful to be competing in the dry heat here in Vegas. Where are you traveling from?"

"Hi, I'm Courtney. I'm the Miss contestant that created the gardening kits for kids in Uganda. How are you enjoying your experience with the pageant so far?"

The Conversation

Your Legacy Project is what you will promote throughout your entire year. Sometimes it's in conjunction with the pageant's platform and sometimes it's a personal platform. Either way, you want to get into the habit of interjecting this whenever possible.

Examples:

"One thing I'm excited about is..."

"...connecting with clubs and community organizations who are seeking speakers on the topic of healthy lifestyles..."

"...interviewing hospital volunteers on their greatest struggles..."

"...getting the word out about my free online fitness program..."

"Do you know anyone that would benefit from this type of project?"

The Connection

"Would it be okay with you if I followed up with you about this after the event? What's the best way to reach you?"

The Close

"Thanks so much for your conversation. It's always nice to meet great people at these types of events!"

It's truly that simple, but it does take practice thinking off the top of your head without the worry of feeling judged. If two humans get on an elevator together, they should absolutely interact! If a pageant girl is in there, everybody better leave feeling glittery!

The elevator introduction is a great tool for networking. Of course, it doesn't have to always take place in an elevator. This quick introduction can be impactful at career fairs, charity galas, vacation getaways, and airports, really anywhere you want to leave a lasting impression.

52: 2 Ways to Get Feedback from Your Judges

WinAPageant.com/52

When I judge a pageant, I always keep a list of suggestions for each contestant in hopes she cares enough to ask. But sometimes pageant women feel too embarrassed or like they're stepping out of line asking for feedback.

In this lesson, I'll teach you two specific ways to get valuable feedback from your pageant judges after the pageant. These approaches have helped me to receive feedback from judges in person, via email, and over the phone. I've even maintained relationships for ongoing help with mock interviews with some of the people I met when they first judged me.

Be warned – asking for feedback can open a can of worms if you don't have a grain of salt for every point. Remember that pageantry is a subjective sport. There are no cut-and-dry rules to winning; it's mostly based on the opinion of a panel of five strangers. Even so, if you're lucky enough to have an experienced panel, you may be lucky enough to get some powerful feedback – even if you didn't win.

Immediately after your pageant, it can be so tempting to approach a judge and ask for feedback. If you are so lucky as to have a moment with your judges taking photographs with the newly crowned queen, this is not the ideal time to solicit their feedback.

Every pageant is different. I know that some directors forbid you to talk to the judges, others host cocktail parties before the pageant and invite the judges! Some directors are stingy with judges' information; they don't want you to reach out to them for fear you'll bother the judge and make the pageant look bad. Other directors welcome the thoughtfulness of contestants to send thank you notes to their judges – especially volunteer judges! After every one of my pageants, I ask the director for mailing addresses of each of the judges – I only ask once in case they are uncomfortable or have a fear-based mindset. If they don't release the information to me, I do some of my own research. It's

74

generally pretty easy to locate contact information when you have the names of your judges.

There are a few ways to go about showing true gratitude and receiving genuine feedback. The first is the simple ask, which is best executed in person. The second is the pen-pal approach.

Approach #1 – The simple ask begins immediately after the pageant. If you have the opportunity to show your gratitude during the post-pageant photos, or in the parking lot afterward, start by saying, "Thank you for taking part in our pageant." Maybe strike up a conversation about where they are from, their family, or their pageant history. If they are receptive, you could ask them if they might be willing to provide some candid feedback to you in a few days that could help you in your pageant career. If not, still wish them well and let them know they are appreciated. If they agree, ask them what the best method is to contact them. Sometimes they'll spout out a few tips right then and there. Or they may give you an email or phone number. Follow up the very next day while it's still fresh on the judge's mind.

Be prepared to take anything she says with a grain of salt. Remember, you are only getting one person's subjective opinion about what they saw for 40 seconds, 24 hours ago. This is not your coach, your friend, or your mom, so don't expect it to come out perfectly or even worthy of application. Though, if someone were to be gracious enough to give you feedback – helpful or otherwise – it would be appropriate to follow up with additional gratitude. Sometimes that means a small gesture of appreciation like an Amazon gift card or handwritten note.

Approach #2 – The second approach ends similarly, but starts with a handwritten thank you note. Show your gratitude for them coming to the pageant, taking time away from their family, spending the day indoors, and fairly judging your performance. In that note, you could mention that you plan to continue competing and you'd be grateful if they would share any helpful feedback that could improve your performance in the future. Give your email and phone number so you are easy to reach and offer the feedback to be "off the record" if they'd like to jump on a quick call.

Think of the last time you approached a judge for feedback. Did you make it more about them or all about you? People want to feel good about their time and value. The more gracious and respectful you are, the more generous and respectful they'll be.

CHAPTER 4

CREATE A POWERFUL PLATFORM

48: The 6 Things You Need to Know for Your Pageant Platform

Even if your pageant doesn't have a platform requirement, you should still have a platform. Your platform serves as your vehicle for media and appearances all of which promote the pageant so it's vital to your experience.

I'm going to share with you six tips to consider when you create your pageant platform. The last one is the absolutely most important one and honestly, the one that most women do not do, which is why it can make the difference between your win and your loss. Still, read the others first so that the final one makes sense.

Element #1 – Unique and Open-Ended

One major downfall of platforms is that they have to be related to an already existing organization. My preference is to not tie a contestant's platform with a specific organization. In my experience, you can sometimes limit your reach when you are representing just one organization. If your platform is generically "America Heart Association," there could be more red tape when you want to partner with local gyms for a heart health event. Instead, I recommend a personalized platform that provides greater flexibility and ultimate reach.

Element #2 – Brand Connection

A contestant's platform must relate to her brand. If you don't know your brand inside and out, don't try to think up a platform. Without a brand identity, your platform appears lack-luster and inauthentic. When your platform and your brand align, suddenly the judges feel an immediate connection to you even in a very short interview time.

Element #3 – Legacy Project

Every reliable and intriguing platform has a product or project based on the contestant's personal brand, which requires her to set it up, but not to manage it. This allows it to last far beyond her year of service. I call this the Legacy Project because this is the goal-oriented incarnation of her platform making real change to leave a legacy. For example, some of my clients have sparked social media movements, developed kits for school children, written useful and meaningful books, and even created businesses around their projects. When you have something this powerful, your interview flies with ease and confidence because the judges are genuinely interested in a project you've already begun to implement.

Element #4 – Marketing

Platforms are like businesses and must be marketed to the masses with a clear strategy that is easily communicated to the judges. If you can't answer the question, "How will you market your platform?" outside of talking in the schools and on Facebook, then you don't have a marketing strategy. Get together with your coach to create an actual strategy to raise awareness of your cause. It should be tied to your Legacy Project, or the keystone piece of your platform, and it should be able to cover more ground that just you as a single person. Think outside the box of pageantry and start thinking like a wise entrepreneur.

Element #5 – Focus On The Light

Platforms should be something people want to talk about. Instead of focusing on the shadow side of a cause, focus on the light. For example, instead of "combatting bullying" focus on "being a friend." Instead of "domestic violence awareness" focus on "creating a healthy home." By simply shifting the focus to the light side of any issue, you invite conversation with anyone, especially the ones that need to hear it the most. Imagine discussing "child abuse" with an abuser. That's a tough topic. But "healthy parenting" would likely be much more welcoming.

Element #6 – Implementation

Platform implementation is so important! When someone says they have a good idea, I'm happy for them, but not interested in hearing about what they *will do*. When they say they've created something great, now I'm interested in hearing what they *have done*. There are lots of good ideas, but not a lot of dedication to making them a reality. The key to your platform is to go out and accomplish what you desire. Don't just create a bunch of plans and expect to win the crown without having implemented. Be more than a dreamer, be a doer.

89: 5 Steps to Figure out Your Platform Legacy Project

WinAPageant.com/89

An awesome platform is vital to getting appearances, especially before you win a big state or national title. Your platform gets you in the door for appearances and media interviews. And when it comes to pageant week, what you've done with your platform is what separates you from all the other contestants. My clients are trained to market what we call a Legacy Project – it's the product or project you lead that uses your unique skills to creatively solve a problem. One of my clients wrote a children's book that teaches adults how to read to children while entertaining the kids. Another created a DIY home garden project in conjunction with Home Depot. I developed a professional home fitness video series available online for free. Whatever you DO with your platform will be your legacy. You don't want your legacy to be that you did nothing.

In this lesson, I'm going to give you five steps to figure out what your Legacy Project can be. We're going to find the intersection between your uniquely amazing qualities and the problems you want to solve.

Step #1 – Write a list of all the things at which you excel. Maybe you are great at cooking or sewing. Maybe you can sing opera better than a professional opera singer. Maybe you know how to talk a cat out of a tree. Whatever you are excellent at, write it down. For me, I knew I was excellent at speaking on camera, designing home workouts, and marketing things online.

Step #2 – Cross off the stuff that you aren't really excellent at. If you can sing, but you aren't the best in your choir, scratch that off. We want to only focus on where you excel above the others. You may end up with about five to eight things on this list.

Step #3 – Determine the group of people you want to help. Who is it you are most passionate about impacting? Is it children who have lost a parent? Or abused pets? Maybe it's adults who want to overcome addiction, or teens that are bullies. Write out the characteristics of this person. If you know of an actual person that fits this category, consider their characteristics. Maybe you'll say, Heather who is the biggest bully in the 8th grade. Or Sam, your friend's dad who has struggled with alcoholism for years. Identify exactly whom you want to help. For me, I chose to help people who weren't exercising, but they really wanted to lose weight.

Step #4 – Make a list of the biggest struggles, challenges, and setbacks that the people you want to help are facing. What is their biggest problem? What are they most afraid of? Maybe the bullies are scared other kids will not like them. So in turn, they pick on other kids so those kids won't be mean to them. Maybe the struggling addict doesn't know how to break the cycle or where to go for help and feels like if he goes to the AA meetings, he'll embarrass his family. For me, the people I wanted to help were embarrassed to go to the gym and be seen as overweight, so they wanted to work out at home first. They couldn't afford a personal trainer or they lived too far from a gym to go every day. They also didn't know how to exercise or which exercises to do in what order.

Step #5 – Go through all of the biggest problems from your second list (step 4) and use your first list (step 1) to create a unique solution to each one of the problems. Get really creative, think outside the box. Don't be held back by time or money at this point. You can work through the details later. Right now, just let your imagination fly! Some will be better than others, for sure, but this is just meant to help you discover where you can use your unique skills to creatively solve a problem. This is how I decided to create home workouts available for free online.

When you've struck gold, you'll know it! Read back through all of your ideas and select any idea that you think is totally magical. That is where the treasure lies for you and for all the people you're about to help. Your Legacy Project won't be easy, but it will be life changing – for you and everyone you are able to impact!

23: Your Legacy Project is Your Winning Ticket to the Crown

WinAPageant.com/23

When I first started competing, I quickly learned that a common on-stage question is "What will your legacy be as the titleholder if you were to win tonight?" I, like many pageant contestants, learned this the hard way – on-stage, instead of at rehearsal. So, naturally I made up some blah-de-blah about being nice and stuff. Then, I had to tuck my tail between my legs and slide off stage.

I can honestly say, I had no idea what to do with the crown if it had been given it to me that night. It wasn't until several years later that I finally realized I was responsible for leaving a legacy. You may be surprised how many contestants on any given stage have no clue what they would do if they won. They think it's like becoming a fairytale princess, marrying the prince, moving into the castle…then what?

Legacy Project is a term I created when I realized that this idea of designing a personal brand and then developing a project to compliment the brand is what truly wins the pageant. Plus, the "legacy" question makes many contestants nervous because it seems so large, but vision is what separates winners from beautiful pageant contestants.

When I first started competing, I was like many of my clients who believe that pageants are won on looks. And that's because the majority of what is seen is the on-stage portion. The audience doesn't see all the work that the pageant winners put in prior to their winning. The work is done behind the scenes, many months prior to the pageant, but the audience only sees the on-stage question. It's really a shame because women then enter pageants without a Legacy Project, and they really have no chance of competing against a woman who has had proper guidance toward an impressive Legacy Project.

Imagine if you were to attend a pageant where each girl gets some version of the "legacy" question on-stage such as:
What will your legacy be?
How will you be remembered?

What do you plan to do during your year?

What impression will you leave on the community?

It happens all the time. The answers that come out are similar to mine that first time on stage. It's some version of, "I want to be remembered as a nice and friendly titleholder. Even if I only touch one life, I will consider my reign a success because every individual counts. I'll do lots of appearances and make the community a better place...blah, blah, blah."

Now, if you are an easy talker and not nervous then this answer can still come off poised and lovely.... it's just that when one of my clients walks onto the stage and has a wham-bam answer that speaks to her Legacy Project, she blows the competition out of the water with something such as this:

"As an advocate for children's exercise, I recently published a fitness DVD for children. It's currently available on Amazon and paid YouTube – the proceeds go to our partner, The American Heart Association. As Miss Titleholder, I'll work with the administrators of the national public library system and the AHA to distribute the DVDs to libraries and school in our community. I want every child to love fitness with a passion – I can't wait to leave a legacy of health."

I mean, as a judge, how can you not give this girl the crown? You'd be crazy – she's the only one with a concrete plan, connections, and a project already in the works. She's clearly ahead of the competition. Plus, she will be poised because she's not nervous. She's confident because she's been thoughtful in preparing this and working with this project. She knows her stuff!

This is why you need a Legacy Project! Because if you are competing in a competitive pageant, all the girls will be gorgeous with an amazing wardrobe, great hair, and lovely nails, but this is not who wins. Who wins is the woman who is able to accurately communicate how she is able to combine her personal passions with her strengths to develop a unique product or project that supports a greater cause.

Your Legacy Project has to be something that can continue to bless people even when you aren't the titleholder, and the pageant can continue to get props for your work even after you give up your title. It's a win-win for every party involved.

Here is the process I use when I work with my clients to prepare their Legacy Project.

Step #1 – Self Study. Your first step is to understand who you are: your strengths, core values, passions, skills, and education – all of who you are.

Step #2 – Dreaming. Step two is to dream up exactly what you hope for the world – big picture style! What is a huge vision that you'll need partners for? Proverbs 29:18 says, "Without a vision, people perish." My version of this says, "Without a vision, pageant girls don't win." But with a vision that is larger than you, God can step in and help make it amazing! So create a dream that is far beyond what you could do on your own.

Step #3 – Partners. Create a list of partners that can help you make this vision come true. Start reaching out – some will be on board and others will not have a clue what you're talking about. This is a great opportunity to practice speaking about your vision with specific outcomes – numbers, dollars, and percentages. Maybe you want to increase donors, or scholarship dollars, or decrease the percent of hardship or increase the percent of participation in your related cause.

Step #4 – Communication. It is HUGE that you know how to communicate your vision through your Legacy Project. So get clear on what you are doing, who is involved, and how it will look in the end. Of course, you also want to communicate how this project will help the pageant promote its cause and leave a legacy of greatness as you relinquish your title next year.

Your Legacy Project shouldn't require you to deliver the content live; instead you want it to be accessible anywhere, anytime. People will be talking about your contribution for years to come. That is a powerful legacy!

66: The Perfect Outline for Your Pageant Platform

WinAPageant.com/66

All pageant women need a platform, even if it's not required. Your platform is the vehicle that gets you appearances and media coverage, helps you stand out from other contestants, make connections to grow your network, and it's the way you're able to leave a legacy during your year.

Some pageants require a platform and even an essay or statement that explains your take on a given topic. Most women who compete in pageants are smart and studious, so writing an essay isn't the difficult part. What's hard about the platform component is two-fold: making your stance different than the next girl and explaining your platform in a succinct way. In this lesson, you'll learn how to actively differentiate yourself from the pack by explaining your platform in a way that is simple, memorable, and powerful.

You may know how it feels to discover that another contestant in your pageant has a platform that is similar to yours or is supporting the same general cause. I often hear that pageant women get worried about this because they think that supporting the same cause means having the same platform. The confusion happens because untrained pageant women sometimes say their platform *is* the cause, "My platform is the America Heart Association." It's a rookie mistake. The America Heart Association is an organization that you support, that is not your platform. If two women claim their platform is the America Heart Association, now we're really in trouble because the judges won't see the distinction either.

You're going to create a unique stance of what you believe, even if it's tied to an organization. If you go through the steps I outline here, not only will you be able to write an essay that is unique and descriptive, you'll also be able to explain how it's different from others to the media, your judges, and potential sponsors.

I call this the Perfect Pageant Platform Outline because it's simple, real (not exaggerated), and will differentiate you from the competition.

You'll have to turn on your creative brain for this exercise, but it'll be fun!

The Perfect Pageant Platform Outline consists of five questions. The answer to each question becomes a paragraph in your essay. Depending on length, you may combine some of the paragraphs, but you should still have five distinct parts in this order.

The five questions of the Perfect Pageant Platform Outline are:
#1: What is the problem from your perspective?
#2: What is your creative solution to this problem?
#3: What are you currently doing to implement this solution?
#4: What impact is it having?
#5: What more will you do when you win?

At first glace, this outline isn't going to seem special. If you were careless, you could easily flash through each of these and come up with a decent essay that could pass, but wouldn't get you to the top. Instead, I want you to pay attention to the specifics that I'm about to review with you and the process for making this unique.

Question #1 – What is the problem from your perspective?

The key to this question is "from your perspective." Incorporate your unique insights and perspective to how you see the problem. Usually, you're view of a social issue comes from personal experience. Tap into your past experiences to be honest about what you are noticing. For example, if the cause you are supporting is childhood obesity, be clear about the problem from your perspective. Maybe you are a teacher at a school where physical education class time has been cut. Maybe you're a mom and your child is asking for cookies and fruit rollups to take to lunch instead of the carrots you're packing. Maybe you were an obese child because the school lunches weren't nutritious. Whatever your perspective, it is yours and that makes it unique, so talk about the problem from your perspective.

Question #2 – What is your creative solution to this problem?

In the second question, you are asked to provide a creative solution to the problem. The key here is "creative." If you give the same solution that the American Heart Association is already giving, then that isn't bringing additional value to the cause. Plus, your perspective is unique, so your solution ought to be too. You may say the solution is to teach other mom's which healthy snacks they can put in their kids' lunches. Maybe you want to raise funds to give to your local school for healthier cafeteria food. Maybe you want to lobby to get physical education classes back in the schools, or create an after-school program to keep kids active, or make an exercise game that families can play together on the weekends. Make sure your solution is creative, and offers a specific solution to the specific problem you mentioned.

Question #3 – What are you currently doing to implement this solution?

For the third section, share what you have already done to test your solution to the problem. This is where most contestants get lazy. They don't want to actually solve the problem. They just want to be a spokesperson for other people to solve the problem. This paragraph will separate the doers from the dreamers every time. If you haven't taken action yet – go for it! I'm certain that you have a really great idea of what you can do to make a lasting impact – implement it! Start the after school program, make a list of healthy foods to give out to your child's classroom – take action! Then, you'll have tons to talk about in this paragraph.

Question #4 – What impact is it having?

My clients are always surprised when they take massive action and gain massive results. It's fun to hear their excitement when something takes off, but it's no surprise to me. That's how it works. When you find a solution and then implement it, you'll attract the people who have the same problem you noticed. They'll be so grateful for you and your solution. You may help hundreds of teens lose weight by creating a teen-friendly food analyzer app. You'll get the attention of local legislators who pass a new law banning junk food in high school vending machines. When you take action, something amazing will happen and you'll want to talk about it in this paragraph.

Question #5 – What more will you do when you win?

In this section, explain your greater vision. Describe how you'll be able to grow this initiative when you receive the title. Don't be vague with 'speaking to the schools' and 'raising awareness to a wider audience' – everyone says that; it's not unique. I want you to be specific and think big. Maybe you'll be able to partner with the national platform organization to bring your list of healthy snacks into schools nationwide. Maybe you will be able to get the attention of more government officials, or promote your program to a new market.

Every pageant woman should have the answers to these five questions. This will help you write your essay, nail your interview, impress the media, convey your message to sponsors, and of course, differentiate yourself to your pageant judges.

CHAPTER 5

NAIL YOUR INTERVIEW

74: 4 Pageant Interview Myths and How to Avoid Them

WinAPageant.com/74

If you've been searching for training to help you win your pageant, or if you have tracked the success of other pageant women, you know of the power that your interview has to not only win over the judges but to win the whole pageant. Maybe you've even sat on a panel as one of those judges and were wowed by a contestant and excited to choose her as the winner.

So, why does the idea of pageant interview make you nervous? It's usually one of these three reasons…

- You don't mind putting in some effort, but you hate watching the news and studying current events.
- You love the idea of making a genuine connection, but doubt your ability to communicate what you really want to say.
- You're great at talking to people, but as soon as it's an "interview" you clam up.

Pageant women (like you and me) don't have the luxury of throwing away a single second of the interview. It's so short that you have to maximize every moment. If you've ever done a pageant interview before, you know that scary feeling of not knowing what the judges are thinking or how you did until finals. You have to find a way to know what you're doing is the right thing and that your strategy works.

In my experience, I've found that four major myths are to blame for that awful pit-of-the-stomach feeling that you get before your interview that leads to no crown at all. I'm going to debunk those myths for you and show you how to replace them with truly effective strategies that will actually reward your hard work and have you blowing kisses from stage in your new pageant crown.

Myth #1: Interview is a natural skill (and not a trained strategy).

What most pageant women think of as the "interview phase" is really just a small fraction of what they really entail. Most women view interview as just showcasing your personality naturally. In fact, the personality aspect is really only about 20% of an entire, well-designed interview strategy. A truly effective interview strategy involves four Key Stages (preparation, planning, performance, practice), all of which MUST be executed in perfect harmony in order for judges to see you as someone worthy of the title. In short, your interview isn't an isolated phase of competition, but the major component to an entire system with many moving parts, specific goals, and subtle characteristics to pull out at just the right time.

My pageant interview system is so much more than just a list of questions with exciting answers. Specifically, my interview system includes strategic development of all elements of the pageant from myself and the judges to the pageant mission itself, all coordinated around my personal themes and story development. It also includes a leadership style to guide the judges, communication skills that develop connection, a focus on pageant marketing and collaborative planning with consistent actions, and so much more.

When everything lines up perfectly, you suddenly grab hold of a simple, effective game plan that becomes the foundation of your pageant competition and gives you the opportunity to perform consistently across all phases of competition.

Myth #2: Interview prep is a ton of effort and super confusing (and that's why everyone's nervous).

Okay, interviews aren't easy. But that's not why everyone's nervous. In fact, the only women that are nervous are the ones that haven't prepared properly. Your interview can be simple when you have the right A-Z game plan that leaves nothing to chance. From the best ways to articulate your greatest strengths to knowing exactly how to respond to the toughest questions, a step-by-step blueprint can take an otherwise complex strategy and make it achievable for even the busiest pageant woman.

The woman that has such a game plan is not nervous. Plus the fact that everyone else is nervous and confused gives her a huge competitive advantage; she has the unique opportunity to be the BEST in comparison to every other contestant since she has the keys to confidently nail her interview.

Yes, executing a pageant interview strategy requires effort, but you've already proven that you're willing to put in effort. You just want to be sure that all the energy you put into this plan will not be wasted, but will lead you closer to the crown. What you can't afford to do is waste time and energy continuing to "figure it out" on your own through Google searches, watching the news every night, and practicing a zillion questions. Which leads me to the next myth…

Myth #3: I'm fine. I'm a people-person and I practice questions all the time.

While it's really great that you enjoy talking to people and are willing to practice, that very same effort could easily become a major harm to you and your performance if you fail to understand the many factors that go into an interview:

- You are responsible for leading your interview.
- How you end your answer is more important than how you begin it.
- Your emotions could throw you off.
- Sticking to your themes will enhance, not distract.
- There are things you may have been taught to say or do and now those things make your judges want to dismiss you from the room.

Hint: It's not enough to just practice questions over and over or memorize answers to the most common questions. There are very specific things you must do to make sure your judges head in the right direction, trust you, and like what you're saying. When you add it all up, it's not safe to just keep practicing questions over and over if you want to succeed in the interview room.

Myth #4: It's too late. My pageant is only a month away.

Okay, maybe you're too late for past pageants, but you aren't too late for this one! With a step-by-step game plan of exactly what you need to do, you can easily nail your pageant interview in only four weeks. Of course, you'll need to put in the work to make it a reality, but I promise your work will be worth it! My hope for you is to avoid the many traps that make pageant interview an epic disaster, and instead learn to interview with confidence.

I have competed in pageants for over 10 years and have made many mistakes along the way. You don't need to do the same. I've compiled a list of three of my biggest pageant interview mistakes over the years and how to avoid them before your pageant interview.

I created a special guide to supplement this lesson that covers the *Top 3 Rookie Mistakes* that pageant women make in their interview. You can get this inside the Beauty, Truth and Grace Guidebook available for free at: WinAPageant.com/Guide.

5: 3 Things To Make or Break Your Pageant Interview

In your pageant interview, the judges are expecting you to be prepared to communicate your best self. The responsibility is on you, not on them, even though they are the ones asking the questions. That means whether it's 20 minutes or 2 minutes, you have to be in control of the values you want to communicate, the stories you want to share, and how you will make an impact as the new titleholder.

When you are in control of your interview, you're able to steer it in the direction you want to go. To be successful, you have to know where you want it to go. You've experienced this before, I'm sure. It's a lot like meeting a cute new guy and wanting him to know how cool it is that you are bilingual and spent a year living in Europe. You find yourself steering the conversation to all things European. You order your coffee with an Italian accent. You tell a story about your old apartment in Paris. If you drop enough hints, eventually he'll ask you to tell him more about it. This is exactly what I want you to do in your interview.

There are three specific ideas to communicate during your interview that will help to communicate who you are to the judges. You can prepare and practice these in advance so that you have an incredible interview and feel confident that you communicated your true self.

Idea #1 – Accolade

An accolade is something that you've done that is really awesome! This proves your success and showcases your ability to accomplish great things. Examples may be if you wrote a book, performed at Radio City Music Hall, or gave a speech to 2,000 people. What have you accomplished that makes you proud?

Idea #2 – Heart Story

Your heart story showcases your passion and mission to make an impact on the world. How will your presence change lives? How has your life changed?

Idea #3 – Marketing Plan

Your marketing plan is a strategic process you've designed to help broaden your scope and exemplify the legacy you'll leave as a titleholder. How can you combine your contacts and abilities to make a bigger impact as a representative of the pageant?

Prepare these stories and steer your interview to make sure you get to tell these. These stories will also be perfect for creating an impact quickly when you are giving a media interview, hosting an event, or talking with someone new about your role as a titleholder.

6: A Recipe for Story Telling

Stories are the basis of human connection. We are able to connect with people through sharing stories and understanding where someone else came from based on what they've experienced. The best communication happens when people know you, like you and trust you. Knowing how to tell a good story is key to getting people to know, like, and trust you.

If you can tell a good story, you'll help others to understand you and feel like they know you. If you're fully honest, your story will align with your actions and that congruence will help people know, like, and trust you, leading to BIG success in your communication.

Good stories are memorable, inspiring, entertaining, and repeatable. They include characters, setting, a challenge, and a big win. Too many details can get confusing, and too little details can be boring. The details should enhance the point of the story and not distract from the main idea. Good stories leave the listener with a knowledge nugget that inspires them. In your pageant interview, you can create instant connection through the art of story telling.

Here's the process to creating a great story:

1. Consider a moment that changed you – Look for big shifts in your thinking and actions.
2. Determine a knowledge nugget – This is the main point of the story that will give your listener something to take away from it.
3. Chronological ingredients – What happened first, next, and last?
4. Cut out the fat – Remove any boring details that confuse or clutter the story.
5. Add some spice for flavor – These are the juicy, emotional details that reveal your personal attributes, values, and characteristics.

6. Let it marinate for just enough time – Use your tone and vocal inflection to let your points sink in fully.

7. Practice – Tell the story to some people as a test and gauge their reaction to see if you told the story effectively to get your listener to the knowledge nugget.

To ensure you can tell your favorite stories in your interview, put the knowledge nugget on your factsheet in an interesting way so that you encourage the judges to ask you a question that will set you up to answer with your awesomely thought out story. Then they will know you, like you, trust you, and choose you to win.

79: How to Lead Your Pageant Interview

WinAPageant.com/79

As a teen and young adult we are surrounded by people telling us what to do, setting boundaries, creating standards and delivering prompts we respond to. We're always being led. Our teachers lead us in school, our parents lead us at home, there's an RA with rules for the dorms, coach who sets up the drills for practice, Miss Gretchen who leads dance rehearsal, and the Pageant Director that tells us where and when to be all week.

It's no surprise that when you walk into your interview, you're expecting the judges to lead you through that process. Don't. This is where it all goes wrong. The judges are not the leaders of the interview room. They are looking for the leader and if you expect them to lead, you will not be seen as their leader but rather just another sheep in the herd.

There are two qualities of leadership that you can employ in your interview room to maintain control and lead your interview. These are pace and direction. Pace is the rhythm and speed that something moves. Direction is the path it follows to get to where it's going. Here's the mantra I want you to use: "I am the Leader. I set the pace and direction." Go ahead and say it out loud so you know you're ready for this.

When I was studying on-camera hosting in Los Angeles, I was trained to use a teleprompter. A script is loaded into a machine that sits just above the camera. As I read the script, it moves along revealing the next line and the next and so on. My first try at the teleprompter was hilarious. I began reading the script and got so excited I started reading really quickly, suddenly the teleprompter was moving at a speed so fast I couldn't even keep up and was jumping over words and skipping phrases. It was a disaster. When I'd finished the script, I asked my coach what the deal was. This is how I found out that the guy controlling the speed of the teleprompter was trying to keep up with me! He noticed I was going faster so he was matching my pace and since I wasn't slowing down, he wasn't.

This is exactly what happens in the interview room when you get nervous and start speeding up. It feels like you hopped on a speeding locomotive and can't find the brakes. Take a deep breath. You control the pace. If it starts going faster than you'd like, you need to slow it down. If it's feeling sleepy, inject some energy and get it going!

The best tool you have is your voice. Use your vocal inflection to control the pace. Long pauses are particularly useful when you need to slow down, and talking just slightly faster adds energy to your words and pace to the room.

The second thing they are expecting you to control, as the leader is the direction of the interview. They don't know everything you want to tell them so don't rely on them to ask you the right questions. Come ready with a handful of answers you want to share and take responsibility for getting them in there. If they are heading in a direction that isn't going to serve you, point them in a new direction. Leaders create boundaries, so let them know if they cross one and get them back on track to what you know is important.

You're already better at this skill than you probably think. Remember a time when you tried to avoid a difficult conversation with a friend. You were great at redirecting the conversation then, right? How about when someone brings up negative gossip about someone you love? You should be quick to correct them onto a positive path and focus on the good.

You are the Leader. You set the pace and direction.

You have to loosen up before your pageant interview so that you can perform in the best way possible. Tricks like imagining the judges naked don't work because it takes your mind off of the whole process. You need your mind on the process to make it work. I want to share with you five tips to loosen up in your pageant interview and connect with your judges.

Tip #1 – Serve, Love, and Give More Than You Take

Anytime we shift our focus to serving rather than being served, to loving rather than being loved, and to giving rather than receiving, we regain a sort of power. It's like being the junior counselor at summer camp. Abuse the privilege and they'll send you home. Be the best darn counselor at camp and next year they'll promote you. Women want to walk out of the interview room feeling like the judges served them the best questions, oohed and awed over all their great personality, and gave them 10's on the way out. Want a 10? Be a 10. Serve them the answers they need. Love their questions as though they are all worthy. Give them your generous approval. Everyone wants to be loved, even the judges. Make them feel like a million bucks and the pressure is off of you.

Tip #2 – Assume the Best

The nature of pageantry makes assumptions run wild. Especially if you don't have formal pageant training or coaching, it's easy to assume all sorts of wacky things to try to explain how you did. Usually, these assumptions come from a place of fear. If a judge coughs when you mention you go to church every week with your Grandma, you suddenly believe he's atheist and you offended him, or maybe you offended him because he doesn't have a grandma. You start second guessing all your values to please someone you don't even know. Stop that. Don't assume anything. Just do you. When we start telling ourselves stories about what we think the judges are thinking, we throw off the interview and the rest of the competition. If a judge is looking out the window during your whole interview, assume she has two lazy eyes that were glued to you the entire time and just appeared off to the side. When you assume the best of people, you react from a place of love and beauty, which is always the most attractive.

Tip #3 – Smile More and Laugh at Least Once

You are the leader. If you are smiling and laughing, they will naturally follow suit. Every girl loves when she makes the judges laugh. And by the way, the judges like it too! You don't have to be a comedian to say something worthy of cracking a giggle either. A light giggle can go a long way to break the tension in the room and make everyone more comfortable.

Tip #4 – Slow Down

It isn't a race. It's more like coaxing a deer at a petting zoo to eat from your hand. You can't overwhelm the situation, but you do have to stick your hand out there with a sweet treat. Everyone has the same amount of time in the interview and if you come off as rushing through the answers or hurrying out of the room, you'll appear anxious. Instead, before you walk in, take a deep, slow breath. Be responsible for the pace of the questions and prepare to use inflection, thoughtful pauses, and welcomed sidebars to guide them into eating out of your hands. Take your time and when they get there, everyone will settle in.

Tip #5 – Practice

The only way to get super-great at anything is by spending more hours doing that thing. Sure, girls win pageants on their first try, but that doesn't mean they're great at the craft. You've heard it said (maybe even said it yourself) that being a titleholder is a job. You have to work at it like it's your job. You have to schedule monthly mock interviews. Put yourself on a media tour. Listen and filter feedback from a variety of people. Train as though you're receiving a degree in pageantry.

Practicing will help you gain confidence and poise when it's time for the real deal.

10: Know Yourself Enough to Win

As a titleholder, you are constantly in the limelight. People are watching you as an example of something they either like or don't like. With great power comes great responsibility, so the judges want to be sure they choose someone that is able to shoulder the responsibility of the title. You must be confident enough in your own standing so that if a wind comes, you aren't blown off course. If you stand for nothing, you'll fall for everything, and we can't have titleholders falling for everything.

Pageantry uses lots of ways to discover your true character. You may have to write a fact sheet that asks things about what you like and your favorite memories and accomplishments. There could be an essay or a community service focus you can choose. You'll likely have an interview with the judges and even an on-stage question that asks something about your favorite childhood memory.

All of these are ways to understand your priorities, values, strengths and character. Once you understand where this is coming from, all you have to do is reflect on yourself until you know yourself enough to communicate your character to win.

The first thing you have to know is that you are uniquely and wonderfully made. This means that the combination of things that make you *you* are unique – one and only. Plus, you are wonderful! You have to own that!

By reflecting on who you are, you'll gain a deeper understanding of your unique and wonderful qualities. I'm going to give you a series of questions to reflect upon to get to know yourself better. I recommend drawing a bubble bath and pouring a glass of something sparkling and turning on some yoga music. Drag a pen and pad into the tub to reflect on the following questions:

Reflection #1 – What do you spend your time doing?

The answer to this question will help you discover your priorities in life. If you spend most of your time at the gym and planning your meals and only a tiny bit of time reading the newspaper, you'll have a clear glimpse of what you most care about. In fact, this is exactly the conclusion I came to in my bubble bath several years ago. I discovered that I hated reading the darn newspaper and watching the news on TV. The negativity always brought me down. That's when I decided I'd just give it up since I didn't like the negativity and drama. Now, I'm able to announce with confidence when someone brings up a current event, "I don't watch the news. Tell me what happened."

Reflection #2 – What informs your life the most?

This will help you discover the values you stand by. For some people, it's the repetitive motto from a parent or a favorite magazine or a beloved movie. For me, it's the Bible. This informs my life most and impacts the values I hold that lead to my actions.

Reflection #3 – What do you know you are great at?

These are your strengths. Don't list everything under the sun. Instead, think about your top three strengths. The way I think of it is that if I had a friend that needed something and it was obvious to the entire group that I was going to be the best friend to help, what would that thing be? For me it's speaking on camera, building confidence in other women, and not changing my actions based on what other people think of me.

Reflection #4 – What are you so bad at that if someone you loved asked you to do it, you'd spare them the embarrassment and hire someone else?

These are your weaknesses. This is the stuff you have to simply manage. For me, it's cooking. I hate spices and cutting things up. So I buy pre-cut veggies and only use olive oil. Every year when I get together with friends for holidays, I tell them in advance that I'll be buying the dish I bring. For weekly bible study nights when everyone brings their homemade treats, I show up with the strawberry and blueberry platter. When you are aware of your weaknesses, you can find a solution to manage them.

Reflection #5 – What do you enjoy so much you'll never not have it in your life?

These are the things you love to do. This is usually an easy one to reflect on. For me, it's going to church, dancing, working out, traveling, and learning.

Reflection #6 – What are the things you can't stand so much that you run from them?

This is the stuff you don't like. I hate cutting tendons out of raw chicken breasts. It totally grosses me out and gives me the heebie-jeebies! But it needs done, so I rely heavily on my husband for this task.

After you reflect on these questions, start to practice putting together a story about each one. You may consider keeping a notebook handy to jot a few other things that are unique and wonderful about you that may be fun to share during your pageant. Keep this notebook handy so you can reference it when you are practicing for your pageant. It'll be good to keep these floating around in your mind right before the pageant so you can whip them out when the time is right.

88: Writing Your Pageant Answers Is a Huge Mistake (Here's What To Do Instead)

WinAPageant.com/88

There are plenty of opportunities for you to answer questions during your pageant – interview, on-stage question, introduction, and pre-pageant media. It can get overwhelming to prepare if you have no specific plan. Most women want to be so perfect, so they craft these elaborate answers to every question under the sun.

It seems like a great idea. Especially if they give you the questions in advance like many pageants do. I was working with a client who was given all 50 possible questions that could be asked on stage. Before our coaching call, she started writing different answers to each question. She spent a lot of time on this and all the answers were truly wonderful. However, when I asked her one of them she would scroll through her long word doc to find her answer.

Don't do that. Writing your pageant answers is a huge mistake! Writing out answers to possible questions will inevitably confuse you, force you to stay within a box you created for yourself, hinder your personality, and drive you (and your coach) crazy.

Instead, I'm going to teach you what I taught her to help you overcome this crazy desire to be overly (and obnoxiously) prepared.

If you get a pile of possible questions, like my client did, first lump them into categories. It's likely they are asking the same thing in many different ways. Make categories like education, platform, passions, family, and memories. I did this for my client and the questions fit into three main categories: 1. Why did you choose your platform? 2. What have you done with your platform? 3. What are your platform goals?

Of course the questions were all different. For example, the question "If you win, what will you want to accomplish?" was in the same category as "If you had $5,000 to spend on your platform, what you would do with it?" One solid answer will fit both of these questions.

When you plan your answers, it's like spilling a box of Legos onto the floor in front of you. If a judge asks you for a blue one, you can quickly grab a blue one. If you don't have the Legos in front of you when you're asked for a blue one, you have to walk to your kid brother's toy chest, dig out the Legos box and then spill it on the floor. Filing through all your thoughts during your interview looking for one memorized answer is equally time consuming. That's how it feels when you get asked a question and you haven't planned an answer for it, or worse, you have memorized an answer that you now have to recall.

You need to plan a story to share for a variety of life categories, not specific answers. For example, let's say that I want to communicate that I raised $25,000 for my platform in a week with a kick-starter campaign. That's the answer. It will work with many different questions.

Question: "If you won, what would you do first for your platform?"
Your Answer: "I would launch another campaign! Last year I launched a kick-starter campaign that raised $25,000 for my platform. I'd plan another launch for six months from now and use every appearance and social media opportunity to get people excited about it so when it launches it would quadruple the success!"

Question: "How would you spend $5,000 toward your platform?"
Your Answer: "I'd hire a kick-starter expert. Last year I launched a kick-starter campaign that raised $25,000 for my platform. I did it all from my own skillset, but with the help of an expert, it's likely I'd be able to 10x that result!"

Question: "What is your biggest accomplishment?"
Your Answer: "My kick-starter campaign."

Question: "What legacy do you want to leave?"
Your Answer: "Kick-starter fundraising success."

See what's happening here? I'm using the same planned answer — not memorized or written out — to respond to similar questions. Most women want to say more, but the key here is to only have a few Legos (answers/stories) on the floor in front of you and each one of them is excellent. When you plan your answers, you prepare enough Legos (answers/stories) to respond with excellence and not be overwhelmed.

This is a game changer in your interview. We spend a lot of time practicing this in the Pageant Interview Game Plan (Interview.WinAPageant.com) because it is the key to directing your interview where you want it to go. When you unlock this strategy, you unlock a whole lot of space in your brain and you streamline your message to make sense to the judges in a very short amount of time.

84: How to Humble Brag in Your Pageant Interview

WinAPageant.com/84

One of the main concerns that some of the loveliest contestants have is that they feel they are talking about themselves too much. It makes them uncomfortable, like they're bragging. They say they are just too humble to talk about themselves. While this is a lovely quality, it is professional suicide.

Sharing your own accolades and being proud of your progress is an important skill in life. When I took my niece college searching throughout southern California, the admissions counselors reinforced what we already know in pageantry: your application and essays have to be more about you than your dog, your grandma, and your mom.

When you attend networking events and people ask about you, what you do for work, and what you're into for fun, they want to get to know you. To be an exceptional pageant woman (or an acceptable college applicant) you have to be able to speak about yourself in a positive light.

The most beautiful way to share an accomplishment is to share credit with others in the form of gratitude. We all know that you weren't the only one that made something amazing happen. Someone helped you, maybe several people. When you speak about your accomplishments, trace your success back to all the people that helped you along the way. Your success puts a feather in their cap and makes them proud.

Sharing credit with others when you talk about your positive points is a great way to humbly brag about your successes. It's a skill that you'll have to practice to master and feel comfortable doing with sincerity and grace.

Here are a few examples:

Example #1 – "Publishing a book at age 16 isn't common, but most 16 year olds don't have the parental support that I do. My parents have encouraged my new initiatives all my life. They certainly are to thank for giving me the confidence to publish at such a young age."

Example #2 – "My volleyball coach has had a reputation for championships. She has taken many teams to states, so when she started to push me my freshman year, I trusted her enough to go all in. I'm glad I did because leading my team to state championships as the captain my senior year is an experience I'll never forget."

Example #3 – "Fortunately, I discovered a program that walks you through all the details of what you need to do to be successful in this area. I just followed the steps with dedication and when you follow a system that works, you see success."

Example #4 – "Everyone has self-control, but not everyone exercises it. I've found that having a personal trainer is what helps me to exercise my self-control. I'm able to ditch the cookies and reach for a salad because I have that added support that keeps me accountable."

Example #5 – "It takes a team to have any victory. Winning Miss World was really a win for my nation. They have supported my progress, forgiven my shortcomings, and cheered me along the whole way. It feels great to stand on this stage with the power of a nation behind me. It helps me know that I don't have to do it alone."

Do you see how each of these examples shares the credit of their success? You aren't fooling anyone when you take all the credit. No massively accomplished person gets to the top on their own. You had the help from people that care and programs that work. Don't shy away from sharing your successes. Give credit where credit is due so you'll inspire others to build a support system that can help them achieve their goals.

63: The 3 Things That Make Every Conversation Memorable

WinAPageant.com/63

As a pageant contestant, you know the importance of being memorable in your conversations, speeches, and especially your interview. You've got to be the kind of woman that leaves an impression on people's minds and hearts. A boring platform speech won't get you to the Oscars and an interview that holds no unique qualities won't be memorable. The key to wowing your audience of listeners is to infuse certain elements into your conversation, interview, and public speeches that will leave a lasting impression and be memorable and valuable to the listeners.

I fell in love with public speaking in high school, and by the time I was in college, I was speaking about once a month, sometimes more. It wasn't until graduate school and as a professional that I really began to hone my skills and study speaking. When I moved to Los Angeles, I signed on with a professional public speaking brokerage and learned so much more as an on-camera host and entertainment professional.

The skills I learned during these moments would've been so valuable to me as a 20-something-year-old pageant woman. As you know, pageant titleholders are constantly invited to present workshops, trainings, and give speeches across their community. The more memorable and valuable your speech is, the more invitations you'll receive and the higher the payment you can demand.

No matter what form of communication, the three things that people remember and value are the same. I'll share with you three tips that can be applied to speeches, interviews, and personal conversations to make you memorable and valuable.

Tip #1 – Insights
When you share something about your audience that they didn't know, you'll blow their mind instantly. Sharing an insight that you know and they haven't taken the time to understand yet will create an ah-ha

moment of surprise and excitement. This is why magic tricks and mind games are so entertaining. They tip our minds on end and show us a new perspective.

Tip #2 – Shareable Information

According to Facebook, the most shared content is the content that makes the sharer appear smart or funny. Of course! We aren't going to be motivated to share something that's ignorant or bland. We want to pass along information to others that we are impacted by in a positive way. Smart statistics and funny stories are things people want to share.

I don't think of myself as funny, so I lean more into statistics and stories that make people feel smart when they retell it or think of it again. When I was competing, the focus of my platform was fitness and health. During my research in the development of my platform, I found that of all the people that exercised regularly, when they were asked what their motivation was to exercise, the majority did not say to lose weight, to be healthy, to get ripped abs, or even to release stress. An astounding majority said these words, "To get a better body." That is why the title and focus of my platform is to help people around the world to get a better body.

Tip #3 – Action-oriented

Actionable content is the most valuable because it allows people to implement change easily and see immediate benefits. The more value you bring to a speech, interview, or conversation, the more you are worth. Actionable steps could be as simple as downloading an app, being conscious of a habit, or replacing certain food choices.

For example, think of the one area of your physical body that you want to tone or strengthen. Now, think of one, easy move that you could do to strengthen that area of your body no matter where you are or what you're wearing. You may have selected your thighs and thought of doing laying leg lifts on the couch in front of the TV or first thing in the morning before you get out of bed. Your simple action step that you can implement immediately to start seeing a result is: do this one exercise every single day for a month. Just the one exercise for the one body part once per day for an entire month. I bet it's more than you're doing now, right? I promise, you will see results. That simple action step is memorable and actionable, which means it's highly valuable. Of course, you can't control who is going to take the action, but it's still valuable for you to deliver.

When you share personal insights, give sharable information, and provide action steps, your communication will be far more memorable and valuable to any audience.

14: Handling Tough Interview Questions

WinAPageant.com/14

Pageant interviews aren't designed to be easy. In fact, I believe they are far more difficult than job interviews. Federal laws prohibit employers from asking questions that could lead to discrimination.

However, pageants are a wide-open space of all sorts of wild questions. Some pageants do have rules for the private interview. For example, Miss America doesn't allow for talents to be performed and Miss International doesn't allow for political questions, unless brought up by the contestant. To know what the rules are for your pageant, simply ask your director if there are any interview questions that are off-limits. Most pageants allow for anything to be asked, so crazy questions sometimes come up. You need to be prepared to deal with them, but that doesn't mean you'll always have a slick answer to every question.

Just as in real life people ask all sorts of dumb, offensive, provocative, inappropriate, and rude questions when you're least expecting it. You have to be prepared to react with beauty, love, and grace.

Some examples of these Tough Interview Questions are:
- Confusing Politics: "Do you think Congressman So-and-So was wise to make his announcement prior to the election, or should he have waited?"
- Personally Offensive: "Have you ever felt insecure about your body weight?"
- Leading: "What kind of mom do you want to be?"

You may have been asked other questions, sometimes they slip out awkwardly, and sometimes they are designed to throw you off. You need to know this truth: you don't have to answer every question, but you do have to respond. What I mean is that you don't have to answer the question directly with a black or white, yes or no answer, but you should provide some reply to at least acknowledge that you're still in control of the room.

There are four methods to respond to a judge's question:

Method #1 – Answer the question directly if you feel comfortable answering.

Method #2 – Answer what they are actually asking instead. For example, if they are asking, "Do you have lots of free time?" you may answer, "If you're wondering if I have time to be a titleholder, the answer is yes. I have structured my future to allow for flexibility so that I can easily accomplish the tasks I need to as the titleholder if I'm selected this weekend."

Method #3 – Ask for more information. For example, "I don't know about the situation you're referencing. If you give me a few more details, I'd be happy to share my opinion."

Method #4 – Respectfully refuse to answer. For example, "I don't feel comfortable answering that question in this setting."

The choice is yours. Remember that you are in control of the interview room, so keep it together and pointed in the direction of your crown.

80: Where to Start to Answer Controversial Pageant Questions

WinAPageant.com/80

Controversial questions are the most dreaded of all. Sometimes pageant contestants tend to believe that the judges are looking for an answer similar to the way they would answer to see if you share their opinion. Even if you don't think that's true (which it's not), you may still be running from answering questions that require your opinion.

What you run from tends to chase you until you deal with it, so you have to look these questions in the face and figure it out. That's what we're about to do. My goal for you is that when you have the opportunity to answer these types of questions, you have the power to positively impact people by speaking hope, joy, and life.

There's a simple elixir to these worries of public humiliation and the catch-22 of controversy: Values. That's it. That's the remedy to your confusion. Your values are the things that you believe are worth something; they're valuable. Your personal values draw a line in the sand to separate the high from the low, the good from the bad, the right from the wrong. Sometimes they help you decide between two goods or two highs or two rights. Values are our decision-making bumpers that help us choose how to live our lives.

If you value time with your family more than you value rugged independence, then you'll go home a few weekends from college. If you value traveling the world more than financial security, then you'll blow your savings on a Grecian cruise with your friends.

Sometimes in our culture, we battle whose values are more valuable than the others. Silly, I know. Like if you value work and I value education, how can we say one is better than the other, right? The answer is so personal; it depends on what the individual values more.

Controversial questions are controversial because there are a million ways to look at it and a bunch of lenses that can shape what we see. When you answer a question that is controversial, you are putting your values on display. It's the perfect opportunity to showcase who you are at a soul level and stand up for your beliefs.

When you say something or do something that goes against your values you usually feel bad about it. The same can happen when you're living outside of your values.

My senior year in college, I was dating a guy who was into hobbies and people that I wasn't into, and I was noticing that it was changing me in a way I didn't like. We'd been together for over a year so it was a shock to him when I did a values list and he wasn't in my top five. I broke up with him and when he asked why, I simply said, "you aren't in my top five." It was sort of cryptic and I'm sure his buddies were like, "she's a weirdo!" My values were not the same as theirs so I was a weirdo to them. I'm glad I got out when I did because as soon as I realigned with my true values, my life was able to take off in the direction of my dreams.

I want you to make a list of things that are important to you. That you'd pay a lot of money to maintain or give up whatever is necessary to keep. Don't just put things like "family" because you think you should. Drill down to understand what that really means.

If you want to identify someone's values, look at their friends, how they spend their money, and where they spend their time. The bible says, "Where a man's treasure lies so too is his heart," which is a fancy way of saying where you put your time, money, and energy showcases what is important to you. You could analyze your own spending of time, money, and energy to better understand your own values. It could help to start with a broad list of 20 things then circle and prioritize the top five (that's how I got rid of the college boyfriend).

Once you know your values, practice expressing them throughout your life. My husband and I have our relationship values printed on a canvas and posted on our living room wall. Every week we discuss how they've shown up in our lives. I know these values and I live them daily, so when a question arises in my life, I can anchor back to these core personal values.

You'll do the same in your pageant. If you know your values and live them daily, then when you get a question that threatens them, you'll be able to stand up for your beliefs with respect and truth.

81: How to Respond When Your Pageant Judge Asks a Political Question

WinAPageant.com/81

Politics are a scary topic in pageantry, mostly because we don't know exactly how we should respond to these questions. Scan the room and tell them what you think they believe? Bluntly give your honest opinion and risk offending others and creating a great divide? Gracefully evade the question all together and attempt to change the topic?

Two most recent and memorable political questions came from the Miss USA pageant in the final question phase of competition. In 2009, Carrie Prejean gave her blunt opinion about same-sex marriage in her top five question and ended up as first runner-up. Chelsea Hardin in 2016 gracefully danced around the question of whom she'd vote for in the upcoming election. She, too, was first runner-up.

I wish I could tell you there is a sure-fire way to answer any question and win. There's not. It's all a delicate dance. What I can tell you is that no matter what, you have to deliver your answer with certainty in what you're saying. Your pageant interview is not a quiz. They aren't so much judging what you say as how you say it.

Remember, you don't have to answer, you just have to respond. Isn't that freeing? Suddenly, you realize, you aren't a presidential candidate, governor, or lobbying activist. You're a student, a teacher, a nurse, a lawyer, a pageant woman – you don't have all the answers, so don't try to be "right."

Consideration #1 – First, success with these types of questions always comes back to knowing yourself deeply and in the context of the greater community. What you say must be aligned with your true beliefs, so speak with integrity.

Consideration #2 – Then, recognize you are a spokesperson for a larger cause. Your voice carries weight because of your association with your platform, organization, company or school. What you say will matter to people, so speak your truth.

Consideration #3 — Finally, know the hill you're prepared to die on. You have to know what you are willing to stand for even if it costs you the title. These values are the ones that make you a powerful woman and influential leader, so speak with conviction.

Remember, life goes on after the pageant. You'll give up the title in a year, start a new career, and the words you spoke back then, when you had the platform to stand for something, will still echo. You may get a difficult question, but seven years after the pageant, whether you win or lose, you'll be able to sleep at night that you answered with integrity, truth, and conviction.

73: How to Show the Judges You're Ready to Win Your Pageant

WinAPageant.com/73

Did anyone ever tell you to use your interview to let the judges know that you are truly ready for the win? Me neither. It was in my third year of competition when someone finally told me that this is a thing. I had no idea that the other women were actually showcasing to the judges that they are ready to take on the responsibility of the title.

It seems obvious now, but it was a shock to me. I suppose from the judge's perspective, just because you are competing doesn't mean you're really ready for the title. In my first three years of competition, I was not ready for it. I still wanted it, but I wasn't really ready to make it worth anyone's while.

Now, from the judge's perspective I know why this is so important. A judge doesn't want to choose someone that isn't truly ready to take on the responsibility of the year because it's not fair to her and also not going to move the pageant forward. Why would they choose a girl who's bumbling around when they could choose someone who's on a path of readiness?

Imagine if you won your national pageant right now and you were catapulted into the limelight instantly. What's your plan to actually succeed? What is your number one goal? Who will you reach out to? What will you say in media interviews? Imagine not having a purpose – wouldn't that turn into an awful year? Then your year as the national titleholder, instead of catapulting your future toward your goals with a solid purpose, would leave you drained of energy, wasting time until you could go back to where you were before all of this excitement.

To be ready is to have a purpose. Let's break down what "ready" really looks like from the judge's perspective. Most women think they have to be kind, a role model, fun or funny, and able to travel. Those are all really lovely things and hopefully you have some of those qualities, but for those of you that have watched women compete for three or five years and finally win, you could surmise that they didn't become kinder or funnier or more able to travel. What they did become was "ready" for their title.

If the judges selected someone who was a nice role model and able to travel, she could end up smiling in front of a bunch of children with her bags packed, but never truly accomplish anything all year. That's not what we want. We want someone who's ready to take on the world, ready to achieve great things and leave a legacy.

Specifically, your judges want a woman who has a clear goal, who takes action consistently toward her goal, and has a plan to collaborate with the pageant title to further achieve that goal. It's worth listing each of these out to help you solidify them in your mind:

- Have a Clear Goal
- Take Consistent Action
- Have a Collaborative Plan

At most pageants, only 50% of the contestants have a clear goal. Even fewer have a collaborative plan, but what lacks most is a woman who takes consistent action. Do all three of these and you are in the top 10% for sure. Let's unpack what each of these looks like.

A clear goal is a measurable outcome that you want to lead others toward. The more specific your goal is, the better. Consistent action proves that you have what it takes to achieve your goal. A collaborative plan ensures you'll go far because you aren't relying on yourself to do it all.

One of my clients' goals is to increase literacy in the home by teaching parents to read to their children in ways that improved reading skills quickly. The consistent action she took was first to write a book that simultaneously taught parents how to read while reading to their children. Her plan as a state titleholder was to do a book tour across all the public libraries and donate her book as she went. She is currently doing that very thing as Mrs. Oregon United States.

Another client of mine wanted to encourage healthy lifestyle changes for people that struggle with healthy food choices. She collected healthy recipes from influential women across the nation and put them together into a cookbook. Her plan was to leverage her title to get in front of more people to showcase these healthy recipes. She did it as Ms. US Universal when she landed a monthly cooking show on a local television station.

Having a goal, taking consistent action, and collaborating on a plan will let your judges know you are ready to use your title to the fullest. Of course, having these things isn't the end of the road. You also have to be able to communicate all of this to your judges in a succinct and meaningful way. We go into depth on this topic in the Pageant Interview Game Plan (Interview.WinAPageant.com).

To get you started, I created a guide sheet titled *The 3 Simple Steps to Answer the Question, "Why Should We Choose You?"* It breaks that question down into three parts to make it simple for you to put this into action. This is available in the Beauty, Truth and Grace Guidebook, which you can download for free at WinAPageant.com/Guide

75: 3 Ways to Stand Out So Your Pageant Judges Notice You

WinAPageant.com/75

When you're competing in a pageant with five girls, it's very different from competing with 50 or 200 other contestants. Getting the judges' attention among five or even 12 contestants isn't that hard, to be honest. But once you get into 16, 25, 50 contestants and more, it can be increasingly challenging to stand out. This is mostly because when you have a group of that size, it's likely that so many of the women have the top five characteristics that naturally prepare them to stand out in their interview.

With 50 contestants, it isn't enough to just have those five characteristics. You have to have a strategy to ensure you'll stand out among the top 10% to get into the top five and win your pageant.

There are three specific characteristics you can display to get the judges to notice you, no matter how many contestants there are.

Characteristic #1 – Preparation

Most women will have done some walking practice and maybe they've spoken on stage before. But there is a big difference between most of those women and the woman that goes above and beyond in her preparation, the one that trains in areas that most other women aren't training. You know that everyone is going to the gym, researching a bunch of questions online, and watching some walking videos on YouTube. You have to get some training like this, but you also need to get the training that goes beyond the basics. You've got to prepare your platform, your game plan for your year of service, how you'll market yourself, and which appearances you'll prioritize. Basically, to stand out, you have to know more and perform more, and you do that by being the most prepared.

Characteristic #2 – Excellence

Most women are squeaking by with what they bring to the table. They try to figure out the least amount of effort they can put in and then they do just that. They figure out how little they can spend on an evening gown, how few mock interviews they should do, and the least amount of weight they need to lose to fit in with the rest of the women. These women don't stand out. They aren't excellent. They just fit in. To stand out, you have to pursue excellence in everything you do. Don't just get some training; get the best training. Don't just wear an outfit that will work for interview because you already own it, figure out what the best outfit is and find it. When someone gives half the effort, they are not excellent. Excellence takes pursuit. No one wins a Grammy without singing lessons. To stand out among so many others, you have to pursue excellence in all areas.

Characteristic #3 – Consistency

Most women try something out and if they don't get immediate results, they give up. Consistency is a standout quality because so few women (especially college-age women) actually have this. It's not your fault. It's just that you are programed to get to the finish line of a 12- or 16-week course and you have to be an expert in chemistry for that length of time. Then you're onto speech class and to focus on speech class you have to give up on chemistry. This is a college problem. I changed my major 15 times in college – talk about lacking consistency. In the real world, however, consistency is reliability. When you prepare for your pageant, you have to consider your communications, wardrobe style, and actions that prove you are able to stick with one thing (your pageant title) that's going to take up a lot of your time for a full year, no matter how exhausted, annoyed, bored, or disenchanted you are. Showing consistency isn't a natural thing that we do, which complicates how you show up for your judges. But when you demonstrate consistency, you will absolutely stand out.

I put together for you a *5-Point Checklist to Know if You Have What it Takes to Nail Your Pageant Interview*. This checklist will make it easy to see if you've got these characteristics. If you do, then you're ready for a pageant game plan. If you don't, then these are the skills you'll want to develop first. You can get this checklist in the Beauty, Truth and Grace Guidebook available for free at: WinAPageant.com/Guide.

24: Stop being so Perfect! You're driving us crazy!

Many pageant contestants believe in order to win, they must project some illusive image of perfection: the perfect hair, perfect nails, perfect teeth, perfect walk, perfect talk, perfect smile. May I just say boldly: That stuff is for the birds!

The reason that pageants get this bad rap is because of their seemingly perfectly poised contestants. They all glide onto stage with glimmering teeth and size 2 bodies. It's hard to not look at them from the audience and think, "She is absolutely perfect."

But when it comes time for her to deliver her on-stage answer to a tough political question or hug a child at an appearance, perfection is not a valued quality. In these areas, on-lookers would rather experience someone who is real, approachable, likeable, and trustworthy.

My favorite illustration of this is from my second year competing at states in Miss Pennsylvania. My sister-queen, Lucy, who was crowned as my peer in my same local pageant, was a spark plug! She was totally hilarious, light-hearted, and everyone wanted to be around her. I, however, was trying to be Little Miss Perfection. I was crossing all my T's and dotting all my I's. "Does this look okay or should I put it a quarter-inch higher? Should I wear these gorgeous rhinestone earrings or these gorgeous rhinestone earrings? Should I go first or should I go last?" I'm certain I was driving everyone crazy.

My sister-queen Lucy was ahead of me in the pageant contestant line up, so she went into the interview portion of competition before me. She came out of the interview laughing and smiling (of course at the time it made me terribly nervous that someone could have so much fun in such a serious environment).

After my interview with the same judges, I left the room feeling relieved that I made it through without too many political questions.

Later Lucy told me the reason she was laughing so much was because she got the most ridiculous interview question! The judges asked her, "What is your solution to the border control issues our nation is facing right now?"

As a perfect pageant contestant, my answer at the time may have been something like, "This is a very difficult issue for our nation right now. Since the beginning of time, any country's main objection is to protect its land with some form of control. I trust our government will find a solution." And the judges would've likely shrugged and moved on.

Not Lucy! Listen to what she said, "What? Really! If I knew the answer to that, I'd call up President Bush and say, 'Bush – I figured it out!' He'd probably give me a million dollars." The whole judges panel busted out in laughter at her very real, approachable, honest, likeable, and hilarious answer. She said what everyone else was thinking, without making anyone feel silly for asking this loaded question. That year, Lucy won the interview award and a good chunk of change!

The truth is, the more real you are, the more approachable, likeable, and trustworthy you become. Think of your favorite celebrities. We adore the ones with whom we connect through their real-life struggles, funny yet human responses to situations, and humble kindness toward others. I'm not saying throw out all the rules of respectability and professionalism, you definitely need to be seen as someone worthy of respect. But Pageantry is all about the balancing act of respectable and real.

When I was modeling in Los Angeles, I had a mentor tell me "Don't hide your flaws. Your flaws will get you booked." It's the little things about you that make you unique and human that attract others to you. You may see them as "flaws" but others see them as real and respectable.

Don't mistake respectable for perfect. I want to share with you five ways to discover if you are trying to be more perfect than real.

You may be 'too' perfect if you...

... wish you didn't have to do all this work to get ready for an appearance.

... have to think before you respond to a question, and then often wonder if you answered the way they wanted you to.

... use your physical or natural human characteristics (which you can't control) as excuses for why you aren't winning: my nose is too long, my chin is too short, my face is too round, my boobs are too small.

... are feeling like you don't belong among these girls or in this dress or with this crown.

... are trying to impress the judges more than you impress yourself.

Real women learn how to do what they must to be professional, but don't try to change who they are. Real women respond based on their values and don't need to justify their beliefs. Real women embrace their natural qualities and seek to better themselves with their health, professional skills, and personal development more than their physical attributes. Real women don't let the imposter syndrome be their focus, instead they embrace the opportunity to grow, connect, learn, and give back despite how others view them. Real women stick to their values and don't compromise their personal truth for the favorable judgment of others.

Listen to me very carefully: if you have done your homework, and you have taken your time to prepare, and you know you are truly suited to win this pageant, then you need to give up the Perfect Girl Gig and start to be a Real Woman. The more real you are, the more approachable, likeable, trustworthy, and respectable you become. That is what the judges are ultimately looking for.

46: Interview Opening & Closing Statements

WinAPageant.com/46

Many pageants invite the contestants to prepare a brief opening statement or a closing statement that is presented during your interview, as an on-stage introduction, or in your on-stage question portion. Since you have time to prepare for this, the judges will expect you to have full control in this moment to help them really understand you in a very short amount of time.

Some pageants don't explicitly say you'll do an opening or closing statement. However, just because they don't explicitly mention it doesn't mean you don't have to do it. I'm going to walk you through an outline of how to structure your statement so you can pack a punch.

Consider the highlights of three snapshots in time: your past, your present, and your future. We're going to unpack each of these and help you create an awesome intro for your upcoming pageant.

Step #1 – Get out a piece of paper. Make three columns and label them Past, Present, and Future. Think about each of these elements as they relate to the pageant and your judges. What are the highlights that stand out in each category of time? Write down everything that comes to mind in the first three minutes. Start with the past and present columns. Then, think strategically about your future. What goals do you want to accomplish, especially as a result of your pageant win.

Step #2 – Choose the best aspects of each category. Get your coach to help you with this because sometimes the ones that stand out are ones you are too familiar with to see as a highlight. Choose highlights that are clear, respectable, align with your brand, and easy to communicate. For example, you may have grown up on a sustainable farm and now you are lobbying for environmental issues and want to help pass legislation for sustainable living. You may overlook the fact that you grew up on a farm even though that's vital to the current story. Or maybe you overcame an illness as a child and you are currently a healthy, productive member of society and want to give others this same opportunity. Do you see? Past. Present. Future. Following the Past-Present-Future outline allows the judges to better understand who you are, what you're about, and how you'll help.

Step #3 – From your brainstorm, come up with a clear personal statement. I usually do this for my clients because, frankly, they aren't that good at it. And you probably won't be either. You're too close to your own situation, so enlist a friend to help you analyze your life highlights and find the thread that connects each of them.

Step #4 – Build out an interview statement, introduction, or on-stage answer within the confines of the pageant requirements. For example, in Miss America pageants you could do a 30-second closing statement at the end of your 10-15 minute interview. After 15 minutes, the judges tend to know you well, so this is more of an opportunity to recap what you (hopefully) already covered and drive home the importance of choosing you for this role.

Even if this option of writing a statement in advance isn't obvious, don't be fooled. You still need to do this! Your opening question in a panel interview and usually every single judge in a private one-on-one interview will be along the same lines just getting to know you: your past, your present, and your future. The more you are able to clearly describe yourself in this brief snapshot, the better the judges will know you and trust you as a titleholder.

For the pageant pro, there are a few more steps to writing this depending on the setting. For example, in an interview setting, you'll want to be more creative with the seeds you plant and not tell the full story so you can set yourself up for some powerful questions, which, of course, you'll already be prepared to answer. We cover this skill called Conversation Loops in depth in the Pageant Interview Game Plan (Interview.WinAPageant.com).

Here is the exact opening and closing I used for my interview at Miss International.

My Interview Opening:
Growing up, each of my parents had a very different relationship with exercise. Seeing where their choices have led them, I believe fitness is directly connected to quality of life. I am motivated to stay fit for my health and I want to instill that motivation in others. As a lifestyle fitness expert and health educator, I've worked alongside the America Heart Association for 10 years, and I've established my own initiative, Get a Better Body, which has already impacted hundreds of lives.

My Interview Closing:
My job as an educator is to help others understand the value of daily fitness. My job as Miss International will be to connect the understanding with the access. My partnerships with the American Heart Association and the International Sports Sciences Association will allow me to create the DVD program that will keep people around the globe healthy for years to come and leave a legacy of connection and health for the pageant program.

I'm not suggesting you copy this, but use it as an inspiration to spark your own creativity. Remember, every time you talk about yourself, you are trying to help the judges understand who you are, what you're about, and how you'll help.

87: 3 Types of Pageant Interview Practice

WinAPageant.com/87

Most women know they need to practice for their interview, but it tends to get confusing on exactly HOW to practice. There are three great types of interview practice for your pageant, which I'll explain here and give you examples for each.

Interview Practice Type #1 – Self Practice

This is practice that doesn't require much effort. It's when you Google around for questions online and then think up answers in your mind. It could also be flipping through pageant flash cards asking yourself questions. It's low effort because it doesn't require that anyone else be a part of it. I believe this type of practice is important. But this alone isn't going to win you the pageant. It's easy to do, but doesn't have much reward.

Interview Practice Type #2 – Real Life Practice

This requires far more effort. This is when you are interviewed by a media station or share a Q&A session from stage as visiting royalty at an appearance. It's real life practice that requires some effort because it involves more than just you sitting at home alone. It requires a plan, an outfit, a microphone, and a whole set of circumstances to support the practice. It pays off too! But still not as much as the third form of practice.

Interview Practice Type #3 – Mock Interview Practice

You just can't beat a mock interview. It takes a ton of effort but has the greatest reward for your success in the pageant because it is a simulation of the actual experience. It gives you the best opportunity to feel the true emotions of the interview process and practice your skills in the exact environment. It takes some effort to set up because there are lots of other people involved. You're responsible to find a location, invite the right people, lead the process, explain it to the mock judges, film it, and thank everyone; it's not easy, but then if it were, everyone would be doing it.

If you want to win your pageant, you have to out-practice to out-perform the competition. A good rule of thumb is to plan a mock interview once a month. After about three monthly interviews, you'll have the process down, you'll know how to distinguish valuable verses silly feedback that you'll get, and you'll be practiced, but not rehearsed.

Not all practice is created equal. It is not enough to scroll through questions online and think you are prepared. Schedule a mock interview to get some experience to increase your confidence.

CHAPTER 6

MASTER ON-STAGE COMMUNICATION

18: Personal On-Stage Introduction

The pageant introduction is often the first impression the judges and the audience receive from the contestant. It's vital that this introduction is authentic and also consistent with who the contestant truly is, and, it can't hurt if it's also intelligent, entertaining, and educational. That can be a lot to cram into 30 seconds. I'll walk you through an easy process to come up with your engaging on-stage introduction.

The full process I use with my clients is to first discover your greatest accolades, choose the ones that are the most important to you and would have the most impact on the audience, find the common thread, and weave it together in a unique, fun, educational, or funny way. I'll explain each step in depth.

Step #1 – Accolades

Discover your greatest accolade in every area of the wheel of life. The wheel of life is a concept commonly used in psychology and personal development. It is essentially a circle cut into pie pieces with each equal piece representing a different area of life including things like family, school/career, personal development, environment, health, fitness, finances relationships, and spirituality – the categories are up to you based on what is a part of your life. Go through each area of life and write one awesome thing you've accomplished in that category. If two ideas come up, write them both, but choose the one you are most proud of or the one that would be the most impressive to others.

For example, in the career area, you may mention the internship you got at a highly respected management-consulting firm. For school you may mention that you were valedictorian. For personal development you may mention that you can solve a Rubik's cube (I can! My brother taught me several years ago – it's a great party trick). For spirituality, you may say you first heard God's voice stand out from other forms of intuition after a 3-day fast (that's another one I can proudly claim).

Step #2 – Top Five

Choose the top five accolades from your list. These could be the most impressive, the most unique, or the most important to you. Don't over-think this part, you can always interchange them later.

Step #3 – Common Thread

Analyze these five accolades and discover a common thread that runs through each of them. Maybe each of these accolades proves your commitment to helping others. Or they are all examples of you thinking outside of the box. Maybe you have overcome challenges in each area. You must dig until you come up with at least one common thread. Usually, my clients and I are able to come up with two to four very obvious commonalities of the top accolades. This is the secret sauce.

Step #4 – The Paragraph

Write a brief paragraph mentioning each accolade and highlighting the common thread. This gives your introduction a theme that can be remembered even when all the other introductions and faces get all jumbled up in a judge's mind. This step will take any old introduction and turn it into something memorable. And, if delivered with zest, this can make your first impression. You have to get creative here. I usually write a phrase or sentence for each accolade and then put a cute beginning and ending to the paragraph and weave the mandatory components (like name, age, hometown) in at the end.

Let me give you an example:
"I'm always one step ahead of the crowd. I finished high school one year early, which allowed me to spend my summer before college learning Spanish abroad. I started my freshman year as the first female on the soccer team. Believe me, it's harder than it sounds. That prepared me to live in Anaheim, CA and at age 19 be the youngest paid

intern at Disney. I hope to be the first female President. But first, I'd like to stand out as Miss Titleholder. With one foot forward, I'm Rachel McKinley."

Step #5 – Trim
After you've crafted the initial draft, trim out the connecting statements and repetition or any unimpressive or unrelated accolades. Practice reading the statement to be sure it meets the time limitations.

Step #6 – Delivery
Practice HOW you say the statement to infuse your personality and make it more engaging and entertaining to listen to. Always rehearse with 10 times more energy than the normal human interaction. On a big stage with bright lights, everything has to be over-done to communicate your energy. Theater participants are great at this. If you find this difficult, it would be great to join the drama club or take an acting class to learn some basics.

Now you have a perfectly timed, entertaining, and memorable introduction. I recommend choreographing some introductions, especially for small children, because it can help them to communicate the emotional inflection of their words. Plus, it'll help you remember what you want to say. Don't overdo this, but a few gestures at the start of each phrase could be useful.

67: Memorize Your Pageant Intro in 4 Easy Steps

WinAPageant.com/67

One of the greatest skills that pageant women learn is to convey memorized material in a way that feels new every time. It's a secret of actors, speakers, and media professionals. And it's a vital skill to win a pageant.

Usually, when a woman attempts to memorize a speech, it generally loses the emotional qualities that make it feel real, relatable, and engaging. One of my greatest pet peeves, and that of every judge, pageant director, and audience member is a boring, monotone on stage introduction or answer to an on-stage question. It's painful to listen to, makes you pity the poor girl, and gets hideously low scores.

I've heard many well-written introductions that get wasted away with no emotion. I want to teach you how to add emotion into your introduction to help you memorize it without boring the audience, but rather spiking their attention and helping them to remember you.

Of course, the first thing you'll do is write your introduction. Once your introduction is written, you'll go through these five steps to add emotion to it so you don't sound like a robot.

For our example, we'll use the following introduction for a fictional character, Erika Johnson. Here is her example introduction: "As a 4-sport athlete and valedictorian, I sure know how to juggle. I even got a scholarship to the circus, well, for basketball. I'm contestant #4, Miss Carlton, Erika Johnson.

Don't underestimate this lesson. Many times, I've worked with women who sound excellent when they are reading their introduction for practice. Then on pageant night, under the lights with 40,000 other things on their mind, sweaty armpits, and barely any sleep, it's not so easy. Trust me when I say, you need to do this exercise, especially if you are in a competitive pageant.

Get out your introduction and print it out double-spaced. I did this full exercise and took a picture so you can see exactly how it looks visually online at WinAPageant.com/67.

Step #1 – Segment out each phrase of emotions. The way I do this is with a backslash between segments. In our example the segments are: As a 4-sport athlete // and valedictorian // I sure know how to juggle. // I even got a scholarship // to the circus, // well // for basketball. // I'm contestant #4, // Miss Carlton, // Erika Johnson."

Step #2 – Go through each phrase and identify the specific emotion you want to infuse into each segment. For example, the first segment "as a 4-sport athlete" I want to sound strong and confident. For "and valedictorian" I want that to sound humbly proud. The "I sure know how to juggle" could be corny humor. "I even got a scholarship" is exciting "to the circus" is embarrassing, "well, for basketball" is sly. "I'm contestant #4" is secretive and "Miss Carlton, Erika Johnson" is confident.

When I do this for my clients, I segment it into many segments. Of course, you don't want to have every word carry a different emotion or the audience will be on such a wild ride they'll be too confused to listen. Instead, you want to tell a story with your emotions. Usually where there is punctuation like a comma or period a new emotion can be relayed.

Step #3 – Now that you have an idea of how you want each phrase to sound practice saying the phrases out loud individually with the intended emotion:

Strong and confident: "as a 4-sport athlete"

Humbly proud: "and valedictorian"

Corny humor: "I sure know how to juggle"

Exciting: "I even got a scholarship"

Embarrassing: "to the circus"

Sly: "well, for basketball"

Secretive: "I'm contestant #4"

Confident: "Miss Carlton, Erika Johnson."

Step #4 – Start from the beginning and say the first phrase with the second until you've mastered the transition. Continue adding a segment at a time until you continue mastering the emotional transition. Do this step while looking at your paper. Eventually, you'll be able to remember your own vocal tone with the words until you can say the whole thing – ta-da!

It's really that simple! This is the method actors use to memorize lines and public speakers use to memorize speeches. It's a simple way to memorize your speech without making it sound monotone. You can listen to this episode to hear my vocal qualities online at WinAPageant.com/67 to give you a better example of how you'll do this.

9: On-Stage Question Made Easy: No More Nerves!

Answering an on-stage question is a necessity for most pageant winners. When you commit to winning a pageant, you commit to answering questions in front of crowds, sometimes hundreds, thousands, or hundreds of thousands. Trust me, the more you prepare, the easier it is. Just like a celebrity prepares to promote their movie on a talk show or a politician is debriefed for a press conference, you too must be prepared with talking points for the public.

Having a process to understand the on-stage question is key to preparing your talking points for your answer. Answers in pageants are much easier than answering the press, so this skill will need to be continually developed as you continue in your pageant career, but the model remains the same.

First, you have to know what the on-stage question is really after. The judges are measuring how well you can craft a full thought and inspire action in a very short amount of time.

My training as a professional host in Los Angeles taught me to speak in sound bites. Incidentally, this is also a great way to get selected for a reality TV show. Speaking in sound bites provides full thoughts in small snippets. The media loves this because they can edit what you said and maintain the context. For example, if the question is "what is the most important idea of your platform," you can't leave your platform out of your answer or your audience will have no context. Mention your platform and keep it short.

An on-stage answer is usually about 30 seconds, so communicating your message at 30,000 feet is ideal. If you get too detailed, you'll have to back out of it awkwardly or you'll over-talk until the bell rings you off stage.

The second element you should understand is that most on-stage questions are all the same. Pageants do this intentionally to level the playing field. Sometimes a girl will get a curve ball, but for the most part you can expect questions to focus on seven main topics: Education,

Fundraising, Awareness, Impact/Legacy, Strategic Plans/Marketing, Opposition/Challenges, and Personality.

For on-stage question, I recommend lumping several of these together. For example, your Legacy Project can include elements of education and fundraising. Your marketing or strategic plan will include elements of raising awareness. All of these will be developed with your opposition and challenges in mind as well as your ultimate legacy. They all tie together. This means that if you can work through each of these, you can create an on-stage answer that is thoughtful and meaningful in advance so you can relax while the other girls freak out back stage. Here's how:

Step #1 – Main Point
State your main point as a story, a statistic, or a new angle on a concept that gets people excited to be a part of. Ask yourself, "why should anyone care about my platform?"

Step #2 – Strategic Plan
Explain what value you bring to the title through your fundraising, partnerships, and marketing plan. Ask yourself, "what am I going to use my title to create during my year?" Also consider your biggest opposition and how you'll handle it.

Step #3 – Goal
Describe your goal to measure your impact and success. It's best to state this in numbers, dollars, or percentages. This is what you'll accomplish during your year. Ask yourself, "how will the world be different because I held this title?"

Step #4 – Personality
Inject your personality into your answer by using dynamic vocal inflection to further communicate with your audience.

Step #5 – Answer

Don't forget to answer the actual question. You'll use this framework to jog your mind and communicate what you need to, but you still have to be listening to your host and answer from the angle they ask from. At Miss International, the questions are historically related to education, awareness, and fundraising. So I crafted an answer focusing on these topics, which pushed the agenda of my campaigning for the national title.

My answer was:
"My strategy as Miss International would be to create strategic partnerships on a global level. As the official spokesperson for the International Sports Science Association, I'll use their film studio to film my Get A Better Body series on DVD and distribute it to 182 countries. And I'll work with The AHA for distribution in the US. My goal is to get more people exercising for a healthier life... and a better body."

To see the video example of my on-stage question that was taken during rehearsal at the Miss International 2014 pageant, go to WinAPageant.com/9.

I always tell my clients, if you want the crown, you have to go through the orientation, the rehearsals, learn an opening number dance, be called into the top 10, answer a question on stage, and hold some other woman's hand while you both sweat until your name is called. It's all part of the game of pageantry. Hopefully these five steps will ease your nerves about the on-stage question.

11: Kill Pageant Patty: Stop Sounding Like an Infomercial

WinAPageant.com/11

Sometimes when you're trying to be poised and articulate, you forget to also be human. When you come off as overly rehearsed, you can sound like an infomercial. This is widely known in the pageant industry as being a "Pageant Patty." It happens a lot when you're asked a question you get all the time or when you memorize your response to on-stage question. It happened to me after competing for a few years. I simply got good at delivering a put-together thought. The problem was that it was void of emotion, which left my audience absorbing nothing.

It wasn't until I began speaking to audiences more and more that I developed this exercise to stop sounding like an infomercial so my audience would better comprehend what I was saying.

To teach these four steps, I'm going to refer to this example answer: "When I first started competing in pageants, I had no idea what I was getting into. I quickly learned that pageants had an incredible power to impact people all over the world. To this day, my goal is to leave a lasting impression of positivity and encouragement."

Step #1 – Break down an understanding of what you are saying

I like to type out the entire paragraph, and then separate it by phrases and sentences. Each phrase or sentence likely carries a different meaning or emotion.

Step #2 – Connect emotions to each phrase/sentence

Give an actual emotion to each of the phrases. With our example, the first phrase "when I first started competing in pageants" might carry the emotion of restfulness. The second phrase "I had no idea what I was getting into" may be ridiculous confusion.

Step #3 – Practice over-doing it with emotion/expression

After I have all the emotions connected to each phrase, I practice saying the entire paragraph out loud using vocal inflection that corresponds with the emotion I noted for each phrase. This can get a little crazy sounding, which is why there's one more step.

Step #4 – Communicate for understanding

In this final step, you even out your tone with appropriate inflection to still convey your message while maintaining the excitement of a dynamic vocal delivery.

When we are used to saying something over and over we forget that there had once been feeling attached to what we were saying. This is a simple process, but if you are un-doing a bad habit, it may take a lot of practice. Stick with it. I promise your future audiences will thank you.

65: Top 3 Tips for Answering the Final Pageant Question

WinAPageant.com/65

The final question can be the most nerve-wracking because in most pageants it separates the winner from the others in the top five. When we're nervous, all sorts of things can go wrong. I want to give you three tips to answer your final question with beauty, grace, and control.

Tip #1 – Flip the power dynamic.

The first concept you have to understand is that most women show up to that final question feeling judged and therefore respond by attempting to perform and create an ideal answer that will make the judges proud. That's not the best way to do it. With this method, you are subconsciously giving the judges the power to control you. You position them above you with greater power. My first tip is to flip the power dynamic. After all, you're the one with the microphone! You have the greatest opportunity to create an impact and everyone is hanging on your every word. By just flipping the dynamic to envision yourself as the one in control of the outcome, you'll instantly clear your mind from all the emotional cobwebs that you'd otherwise have to sort through.

Tip #2 – Flood your thoughts with your essence.

The second tip is to focus on the essence of who you are. Our minds are always full of thoughts, which are generated based upon our environment. Remember when you would cram for a test in college and it worked? The reason you could get an A on a test you barely studied for is because you flooded your mind with the thoughts immediately before the test was taken. You weren't absorbing the information, per se, but it was enough to make those thoughts available to your brain. You need to "cram" for your on-stage question. You need to release everything else that is happening in that moment to focus on your essence: what makes you *you*, including your values, strengths, beliefs, experiences, and goals. When we're nervous, it's hard to tap far into our thinking mind, and instead we pull information from whatever is on the "top" of our mind. Flood the top of your mind with your values, strengths, beliefs, experiences, and goals in an organized manner moments before you walk on stage to answer the question. Practice this method so you know you can do it on a moment's notice in a high-stress environment. Then, everything that spills out will be aligned with your true essence, and that's whom the judges want to know.

Tip #3 – Be honest.

The third tip is simple but crucial – be honest. Being honest is a more concrete way of saying, "be yourself." That phrase "be yourself" is largely misunderstood because it's hard to imagine being "someone else." But what the phrase is trying to encourage is that you be honest with who you are rather than hiding your insecurities and trying to be perfect. No one believes you when you're perfect. "Perfection" is annoying, but honesty is endearing.

The first time I landed in the top five of a state pageant was in my early 20's and the question I received was from a beautiful, mid-30's judge who asked me, "What kind of mom do you want to be?" My answer was a pageant answer. Something like, "I want to be like my mom, very supportive, caring, and loving." However lovely my answer sounded, it was a total lie. The truth was that I didn't even think I wanted kids at that point. I was only in my 20's and hadn't met my husband yet. Instead of just saying that, I peered down at this judge wanting so badly for her to like me that I made up this beautiful lie. In hindsight, I wish I had said, "I haven't decided that I want to be a mom yet. I'm hoping to one day meet a man that I want to marry and I'm trusting that when that happens, I'll feel inspired to have children. Then, I'm sure my mom vision will come to life." If I would have said that, I would have gotten a roaring applause and been seen as honest, trustworthy, likable, and relatable. Instead, my beautiful lie got a sweet little applause and I was first runner up.

I share this story so you know that this stuff happens. I'm not a liar, but in that moment, I wanted to be liked so badly that it clouded my mind and shaped my answer. That is one of the most memorable experiences of my pageant career because it was in that moment that I began to see myself as a unique individual, and I started to speak my truth with grace and love. I never lied on stage again. Instead, I developed a lovable interview personality (all my own, by the way) that was unapologetic and fully in love with who I am.

Flip the dynamic so that you see yourself as being fully in control and powerful. Flood your thoughts with your essence – what makes you spectacular. And be honest.

CHAPTER 7

FUND YOUR PAGEANT CAREER

27: The Price of a Pageant (A Budgeting Guide) – Part 1 Mandatory Expenses

WinAPageant.com/27

There are three ways to do anything: the cheap way, the expensive way, and the right way. You don't have to have a lot of money to do it the right way. Nor are all the cheap ways wrong. There is a balance to strike.

My goal is to share with you my opinion of what I believe works best in pageantry, plus give you several budgeting tips to save money. What I'm hoping to help you avoid is post-pageant buyer's remorse. Buyer's remorse is the painful, sick feeling you get the morning after your pageant when you realize you spent tons of money on your pageant and have nothing to show for it. Before you start to think about how you want to spend your resources, create a goal: what do you want to get out of this pageant experience?

The goal of my first pageant ever was to check it off my bucket list. I just wanted to compete and I didn't really care to win, though I would've gracefully accepted it. I choreographed a cool new dance to perform for talent, I laughed through most of rehearsals with the other girls, and I re-wore my prom dress for evening gown. I put in some time with rehearsals for my dance and the pageant production. But that's really it. I didn't win. But I did check it off my bucket list, so I was happy! Mission accomplished.

The second pageant I competed in, I just wanted to dance in front of a huge audience – this pageant was held at a grandstand with 2,000 seats. I choreographed one of the coolest dances I've ever performed. I practiced close to 10 hours a week on that dance. I had a blast with the girls at rehearsals and nailed my talent every time. I borrowed my whole wardrobe, except for my $45 interview suit from JC Penny's. Then, five days before pageant competition, I decided my goal wasn't just to dance; I actually wanted to win. In the final five days, I was hyperfocused at rehearsals, started asking my parents for any info on current events so I could catch up on the last five years of politics. I practiced my walk, my interview, and the opening number. Shockingly, I won.

I continued competing for a few years with the goal of earning scholarship dollars. Then, I started to realize my impact could be so much larger if I actually won. When I decided my goal was to win, my whole strategy changed. I actually started using a budget. I've since expanded on that budget and broken it into four types of expenses: Mandatory, Expected, Wardrobe, and Miscellaneous.

Don't let your budget overwhelm you. Treat it like a professional would. Allow it to help you prepare. Once you identify all of your pageant expenses, you can identify how to pay for them – for example, you can use your own earnings, the help of friends and family, or maybe sponsors or fundraisers. We'll get into those details later. For now let's just focus on figuring out your specific budget.

As you read these next few chapters, it would be helpful to use the Budget Guide I've create for you to record your expenses. The Budget Guide is inside the Beauty, Truth and Grace Guidebook. Download it for free at: WinAPageant.com/Guide.

Mandatory Expense #1 – Entry Fee

Some pageants don't have entry fees at all. Other pageants cost $2,000 or more to enter. On average, pageants cost about $1,000 to enter. This expense can cover things like hotel stay, meals, pageant week adventures, gift bags, opening number dresses and other elements of the actual pageant.

Mandatory Expense #2 – Program Ad

Often, pageants will have a mandatory program advertisement. When a pageant says something is mandatory, it's generally because it is something that is very valuable to the pageant itself so don't take this lightly. Some pageants don't require this at all, so you can write, "zero" in your budget. On the high end, I've even seen program advertisements for $1,000. On average I'd recommend you estimate about $100 to $250 for this expense.

Mandatory Expense #3 – Platform Page Design & Sponsors Ad Design

Sometimes, pageants offer space to each contestant to showcase their platform in the program booklet. It's sort of like a magazine page advertising you and your platform. I always recommend that these be professionally designed. Sometimes your sponsor will provide their design, other times you'll have to afford it. I have seen people even charge $500 for platform page designs, and that totally blows my mind. I cannot even imagine spending $500 on this. I have some better options for you. First, go through your pageant's past program books for ideas and choose ones that you really like. Sketch a general design of how you'd like yours. Where will you put your headshot, your title, your goal statement, and other images? You could create it yourself using a site like Canva.com or Adobe if you are a graphic designer. Otherwise, either find a designer at your company or in your community that could do it for you or hire someone yourself. I usually go to a freelancer website like Fiverr.com or Upwork.com. You may end up spending $20 after several revisions, but it will be worth it for the quality.

You may have other mandatory elements of your pageant, like hotel, travel, or other fee-related things, so add those to your budget now. Next we'll talk about expenses that aren't technically mandatory, but are still expected.

28: The Price of a Pageant (A Budgeting Guide) – Part 2 Expected Expenses

WinAPageant.com/28

There are expenses in pageantry that may not necessarily be "mandatory" like entry fees, but they are expected of the pageant women that are competing. It's mandatory that you wear a hairnet, but it's expected that you wear deodorant. I don't want you showing up to your pageant having done just enough to get by. I want you showing up like you know what you're doing and are ready for the title.

Expected Expense #1 – Coaching

You are expected to have some type of preparation before you compete. I recommend about 10 to 20 hours of coaching prior to your very first pageant at a local level (if you want to win). At a more competitive pageant, like a state or national pageant, you'll have dramatically more than that. But, start with somewhere between 10-20 hours. Some local pageant coaches charge around $30-50 per hour. That's what I started at. Then, as I got an advanced degree, coaching credentials, and competed all over the US in 5 different systems, I had more clients and charged $75 per hour. Some pageant coaches charge up to $400 per hour. There are ways you can get a lower hourly rate by purchasing multiple sessions or attending workshops. My hourly rate now is $250, but I run a group program with individualized coaching for around the same price. Knowing that you'll need 10-20 hours, you can set your budget according to the type of experience you want.

Expected Expense #2 – Headshot

You certainly could have your mom take your photo, but you are expected to submit a professional headshot. Professional shoots usually include the expense of hair and makeup styling for the shoot. Some photographers charge a sitting fee just to be in their studio, and then they charge per photo you want to purchase. Most pageant photographers charge for the shoot and give you nearly all the pictures.

If you go to a local photographer, you could spend less than $100 on decent photos, especially if you give the photographer a lot of direction on the look you want and maybe hire out for hair and makeup. If you go to a photographer that has experience with pageantry, you'll likely have a much better experience, your final looks will be easier to choose, and your hair and makeup will be spot-on. Though, you may end up paying $1,500 or more. The best deal I've seen for pageant photography with hair and makeup was $800 for fabulous images. You may spend $1,000 or $3,000, depending on how many different outfits you want to put on and how many different sceneries and edited photos you'll receive in the end.

Expected Expense #3 – Tanning

You don't have to look like you're from Hawaii, but stage lights do make everyone's skin wash out a bit. Having a tan is not mandatory, but it sure does improve your stage look. I do not suggest a tanning bed nor sun tanning outside. Instead, I suggest a spray tan, which is what most pageant women do so they can protect their skin for long-term beauty. Spray tans can be $30-70 depending on where and when you get them. Backstage tans will be more expensive than the one you can get in the neighborhood. You could consider applying a bronzing lotion yourself. Some really great ones may only cost $10, but require your finesse to apply them evenly.

Expected Expense #4 – Hair & Makeup

Professional hair and makeup really separates the professionals from the pack. I recommend either taking a lesson for $500 to learn to do stage makeup yourself or hire an artist for pageant week to style your hair and makeup the entire time, which may cost $600 each day. At the very least, sneak off to an Ulta counter and have an artist do your hair and makeup there for just the cost of products.

Expected Expense #5 – Tailoring

Unless you are a fit model for every line of clothing you're wearing, you'll likely need your wardrobe tailored. Maybe your mom or grandma can help you with this, but if you don't have a family seamstress, you'll need to get some recommendations in your area. You'll likely pay $100 to get your gown altered, more if it has elaborate beading. Even a simple hem on an appearance dress could be $15-30. If you don't know how much your tailoring will be, I'd put at least $500 for your entire wardrobe and as the pieces come together, you can adjust that more accurately.

Expected Expense #6 – Autograph Cards

Autograph cards are headshots with information that are used as a marketing flyer and a business card. Autograph cards usually have your headshot, name and your title on them. I like to include information about my platform and social channels on them too. You could design them and print them yourself for very little. My favorite tool for this is VistaPrint.com. Vista Print is a printing company. You provide the design and they print and ship them to you based on your specifications. You could get 100 cards for about $25. Usually the more cards you buy the cheaper they are.

Add any other expenses onto your budget that you know are expectations at your pageant. Then, move onto the next part: wardrobe.

30: The Price of a Pageant (A Budgeting Guide) – Part 3
Wardrobe Expenses

Pageant wardrobe is the area of pageantry that gets the most attention. I want to discuss your wardrobe for every phase of competition so you know what to expect.

Wardrobe Expense #1 – Opening Number

Your opening number outfit can range from jeans and a tank top to formal attire. So the thing that makes the difference is usually the level of competition and how much the entry fee costs. If you're competing at the State level or the national level, then you should expect to wear at least a cocktail dress. Some pageants include the cocktail dress as a part of the entry fee, and you're only responsible for alterations. Others will expect you to buy a specific pair of earrings, order a specific dress, or ask you to find a pair of dark jeans or a red cocktail dress. At the very least, I'd recommend budgeting at least $100 for alterations and accessories.

Wardrobe Expense #2 – Swimwear or Active wear

Pageant swim suits cost about $100-$500 depending on the cut, color, fabric, and designer. Active wear could cost $50 or $200 depending on your style, taste, and designer. You could find something great from T.J.Maxx but might prefer something from Fabletics of Lululemon.

Wardrobe Expense #3 – Fun Fashion

Generally fun fashion outfits are a gown or costume that has been customized and fancied-up a bit to bring out your fashionable style. You may buy a $200 outfit that you add some spunk and rhinestones to and in the end it adds up to about $500. It of course can be done for less, but after alterations, beading, and accessories you'll want to have a budget to play with for this area.

Wardrobe Expense #5 – Interview

This area of competition probably has the largest range of budget. Some outfits can be spectacular with a $50 suit and $20 pair of heels. You just have to make sure that your outfit is spectacular even up close. The stage can be forgiving of certain fabrics and fits, but your interview outfit has to be excellent. You may get a BCBG sheath dress for $150, or a pageant interview suit for $300. Some women go for the $1,000 shoes! It doesn't matter how much you spend, but rather how great it looks on you, up close and personal.

Wardrobe Expense #6 – Evening Gown

Most pageant judges are directed to not judge the gown but the girl in the gown. A great gown could cost $300. If you want lots of beading or a famous designer or many layers of fabric, you'll pay more. Custom gowns can cost $5,000-$10,000 or more. Don't forget earrings for your gown, which can be $20 or $200. And shoes can also be $20 or $200 depending on the designer.

Bottom line: you'll need to set a realistic budget and then do your very best with what you've got. Most smart women don't want to spend $5,000 on a gown; they'd rather spend $2,000 on a gown and $3,000 on their platform gala. Just because you spent the most money doesn't mean you'll win.

Next, let's talk about the miscellaneous expenses that seem to always creep up on you pageant week.

31: The Price of a Pageant (A Budgeting Guide) – Part 4
Miscellaneous Expenses

WinAPageant.com/31

There are several miscellaneous expenses that are no-brainers and easy to determine, but you still have to include them in your budget.

Miscellaneous Expenses #1 – Travel & Accommodations

Sometimes travel and accommodations are taken care of by your pageant, other times it will be your responsibility to plan for in advance. You may not need more than a tank of gas to get to your pageant. You may need a flight abroad with three checked bags. Will you need a hotel room? What about transportation to and from the pageant activities? Think through your pageant week and account for all your foreseeable expenses.

Miscellaneous Expenses #2 – Pageant DVD and Photos

Most pageants sell a professionally recorded DVD and photographs for contestants to purchase. Pageant DVDs average $50-$200 depending on how many nights are captured. I've seen photographers charge up to $900 for a week of raw candid images. I rarely purchased the DVDs in my career and I'm kicking myself for it now. I just didn't value it at the time, but now that would be so fun to watch and look back on. My advice is that you find a way to get at least the DVD for these memories.

Miscellaneous Expenses #3 – Rhinestones and Crystals

Adding stones to your wardrobe is not cheap. If you want to do this, you'll want to look into the cost of the stones, the handwork to glue them on, and the hardware you'll need to do the gluing if you'll be doing it yourself. Swarovski crystals and Aurora Borealis crystals are usually sold by the gross (144 stones). You may be able to get a good amount of crystals for $100 and the glue gun for about $50.

Miscellaneous Expenses #4 – Pageant Week Needs

There are lots of tools you'll want during pageant week: a travel steamer, extra foam inserts for your wardrobe, sticky boobs, band aids, makeup, a tote bag, power strip, long mirror, garment bags, wardrobe rack. Consider what you'll want for backstage and rehearsal week.

Miscellaneous Expenses #5 – Personal Grooming

Consider your personal grooming expenses like waxing, hair dyes, pedicure, manicure, massages – anything you'll need to prepare you for your pageant.

Miscellaneous Expenses #6 – Gifts

I always budget for notes and gifts for my team (sponsors, coach, makeup artist, stylist), the production team (backstage volunteers, pageant directors, production staff), and my fellow contestants. Depending on your style of giving, you'll need a budget for all of these, not just to prepare the funds but also to help you remember everyone involved in your success. I'd recommend something in the ballpark of about a $2-$5 gift for each of your fellow contestants, maybe $20 for your roommate, $50 for each member of your team, and $100 for your pageant directors.

To truly excel in pageantry, you'll have to be prepared. I've done a lot of the work for you by creating this Budget Guide to help you track your expenses. Download it with the Beauty, Truth and Grace Guidebook here: WinAPageant.com/Guide.

26: How to Get Pageant Sponsors

WinAPageant.com/26

As a former competitor, I completely understand how the expenses of pageantry add up. Now, I have to admit that as a pageant winner, the prize dollars of pageantry also add up, so of course that is the ultimate goal. In my first 5 years of competition, I probably spent close to $8,000 – but I made over $12,000 in scholarship dollars.

You will always have to invest something (usually time or money) in order to get something back. Wall Street says, "You don't get a return without an investment. Karma says, "You get back only what you put out." The Bible says, "You will reap what you sow." If you aren't sowing seeds before the pageant, then you won't be reaping a crown.

If you feel strapped from the beginning, you may not make wise choices about your expenses, which could leave you settling for third-rate services, wardrobe, or foregoing necessary elements of pageantry all together.

It's likely that you've heard of other girls getting sponsors for their pageants. Sponsors are usually featured with advertisements in the program book and are often mandatory for each contestant to acquire. Why would a pageant require sponsors? Glad you asked.

The pageant benefits from the contestants having sponsors for 2 reasons.

Benefit #1 – Their pageant is better because the contestants are more prepared through coaching, have great makeup, and a gorgeous wardrobe that they may not otherwise have been able to obtain without sponsorships.

Benefit #2 – If a pageant woman is able to secure her own sponsors, she is a much stronger asset as a titleholder to the pageant itself.

This is part of the reason that sponsors are featured in the program book – to show them gratitude, but also to honor the contestant who is a rock star sponsor-getter! Don't think the judges don't look at that.

But, there's a problem. There are lots of pageant girls out there that can't find a sponsor at all. Or, they get a little $50 here and there, which gets eaten up pretty quickly in just one coaching call.

The best way to search for sponsors is not to find a billion people to give you $10. Nor is it spending your time and energy on a zillion fundraisers, draining the energy of everyone you ask to help, and netting $200. That doesn't even pay for your makeup for one day. I did all of this in my early years of competing and as soon as I learned this 7-step strategy, I landed a sponsor over breakfast for $3,000.

In this lesson, I'm going to outline for you the seven steps to get a pageant sponsor to help you pay for nearly everything. Now, don't get me wrong – these steps aren't easy… there's no such thing as a free lunch! You need a clear strategy to position yourself to be worth a large investment that will pay off for the sponsor more than a tax deduction would.

These seven steps cover three phases. We'll unpack each in sequential order.

Phase 1: "What Can I Offer"

Most pageant women ask for sponsors like a 10 year old asks mom for money for the concession stand at a ball game. Don't worry, I did it for years too because I didn't know what I was doing. Then, when I started approaching it from what I can offer, that's when everything changed. You need to know your skills, your contacts, your strengths, and what you bring to the table. This comes from understanding your personal brand and image. When you know who you are, what you can do becomes way easier.

Step #1 – know your skills and values

Step #2 – know your brand

Phase 2: "What Do 'We' Want"

In this phase, you'll incorporate your platform, vision, and mission statement and then align this with companies that have similar missions, visions, and platforms. It's usually not non-profits. The best sponsors are for-profit companies.

Step #3 – define your platform, Legacy Project, and goals

Step #4 – align yourself with companies that share your values

Phase 3: "How Can I Contribute"

There are three steps in this phase that get you from introduction to follow-through. When you approach a company for sponsorship, you'll use everything you know about them and you to design an unbelievable offer that they can't say no to. If you missed the mark, that's okay. You can adjust it to better align from their perspective. Then, you've got to deliver on your end and impress the heck outta them! Always over-deliver!

Step #5 – propose a deal

Step #6 – negotiate a win-win

Step #7 – over-deliver

Sponsors have what you want: money. If you are asking for what they have, give them what you have. You don't get a return without an investment.

94: Creating a Valuable Pageant Fundraiser

WinAPageant.com/94

Pageantry, if you are performing at a high level is not any different than someone pursuing professional golf or Olympic ice-skating. Any time you want to perform at a high level, you'll have to first commit to an initial investment. In pageantry your investment is in an entry fee, fitting wardrobe, coaching, and a host of other expenses. Your investment is the seed you sow before you reap the great harvest.

Even so, there are opportunities to raise funds to support your dream. You could get a job, find sponsors, or host a fundraiser. In this lesson, we're focusing on fundraisers.

In elementary school, you probably sold candy bars, Christmas wrapping paper, and lollipops to raise funds for various charities and school functions. The most wide spread fundraiser is the Girl Scout cookies. It's hard to resist delicious thin mints and the opportunity to help young girls develop professional skills and support their development.

The cookies are great for small children. However, there are other ways to fundraise – ways that can bring you far more profit in a shorter amount of time with a smaller group of people. That's what I'm going to teach you to do in this lesson. I want to change your mindset from what you may have known in the past. Pageant fundraising isn't about candy bars and bake sales – think bigger! Think more valuable!

First, let's talk about why thinking small is harder than thinking big. Let's say you want to raise $1,000 for your pageant. That's not much in Pageant Land, so it's reasonable to assume you can do this. If you buy candy bars for 50 cents and sell them for $1, you make 50 cents each sale. You'd have to sell 2,000 candy bars to make your goal. Have you ever seen what 2,000 candy bars looks like? Each box usually contains 10-20 bars. Imagine 100 boxes of candy bars! That's crazy! And do you really know that many people who eat candy bars? I remember in school when I'd sell candy bars and someone would buy a box of 10 and I'd think, "WOW I'm rich!" But seriously, I only made $5. I have to find 200 buyers like that to make it work. Do you see what I'm saying? That's the hard way to your goal. I want to teach you the smart way.

Fundraising is a lot like negotiating your salary at work – you get paid in direct proportion to how much value you provide. Candy bars are sold everywhere for pretty cheap. They don't solve major problems or offer lots of value. Therefore, your profit is pretty low. But if you provide something of truly great value, people will be willing to invest in you to receive that value.

For example, let's say you are an artist and you love painting. Could you paint a beautiful canvas of someone's beloved pet and charge more than $1.00? Yes. Have you ever heard of someone doing that in your hometown? I haven't. But everyone I know with a dog would love a custom painting of their pup. Canvas wall art at T.J.Maxx is around $30. Famous artists commission custom artwork for thousands of dollars. Depending on your talent, turnaround time, and elegance of delivery, you may be able to charge $100 for a custom canvas of someone's pet. If you did that, you'd only need to paint 10 pets to reach your goal of $1,000. Do you see what I mean?

You are paid in direct proportion to the value you provide.

If you are a trained yoga teacher, you could host an hour-long Thursday night yoga class at your apartment complex or YMCA and give peppermints out at the end. You could even say it's donation–based, and if you were truly excellent and provide insane value, you'd have a lot of people coming and paying you big bucks! I once gave $50 in a donation yoga class when I first moved to LA because she was that good.

My brother used to write rap lyrics about a family member or friend of his and record it for their birthday. It was so awesome! He loved rhyming and had all the equipment, and he was so good at it! I kept telling him I wanted to start a business with him to sell them – it's huge value and no one else is offering it at such a high quality level, so you can charge more.

Maybe you can help a teen pick out her prom dress, redecorate someone's home, or teach Spanish to the homeschool kids in your neighborhood – I'm sure parents would love that!

The point is that when you get creative, you'll find you are able to provide more value and that is worth more money.

Here's your homework: I want you to make a list of 10 things you can do that bring massive value to others. Think about what you do at school or work, but also creatively – what do you enjoy? Then, for each one of these 10 things think of 1-3 ways you can apply it. Don't rule anything out yet. This is all the brainstorming phase. As you go through this process, it's likely something will jump out at you.

Once you have that ah-ha moment of what feels right, create an outline of how you'll pull it off. What resources you'll need, what examples you have to show your work thus far, where you can find your donors, and what will get in the way. Don't overthink it. This is where lots of people get stuck. Don't get stuck thinking of all the reasons to hold you back. Instead, when it feels right, go for it!

95: Wise Pageant Investments Yield Life-Long Returns

WinAPageant.com/95

There are lots of things to spend money on in pageantry – from wardrobe, shoes, and earrings, not to mention week-of stuff like DVDs, gala tickets, special seating, backstage roses, contestant gifts; it gets expensive. And when you're working from a budget (as we all should be as good stewards of our money), it's hard to know what's important and what's not. I'm going to break down how to choose your investments wisely so you reap a life-long return.

First, you need to know the concept about how money flows. Money is like a river. It flows through people – from one person to the next and through them to the next and so on. If money flows to someone and stops with them (like they are hording it or aren't using it for increase and to serve others), then it will cause a dam in the river and pretty soon the river will re-route to flow around that person, but no longer to them and through them.

When you are part of the flow, your job is to steward the money. Some you'll save so that when you're out of a harvest season you won't become a burden on others. Some you'll give away to help others when they need it. And some you'll invest, which is what we'll talk about today.

God paints a picture of resources similarly. God is our source and everything He gives us (money, time, energy, gifts) is a resource to use for the greater good. Don't be a pack rat with stuff He's given you, or He won't trust you with more. If you want more money, time, opportunities, friends, energy, gifts, and experiences to flow to you (like when you win a pageant), then you've got to learn how to steward what He's given you. If you win your pageant, you are likely to be able to touch more lives and support more people. This investment is important to you, but really important to God since He gave you these gifts to begin with!

When you send some of your money, time, or gifts (any resource) out of your hands, it goes to work for you. Sending your resources out from you is like creating an outlet in the river so that you don't cause a backup that forces the river to go around you. It further waters the land and helps other rivers flow around and through others.

The lesson you need to walk away with here is that sending your money out isn't a bad thing if it's to the right place. When people make financial investments, they seek to improve their financial standing through real estate properties, growing businesses or stocks. They don't just buy what's cheap or what's available; they find what's best and wait until the time is right. When the time is right, they pounce.

When people make educational investments, they seek to improve their education through things like college, Rosetta Stone, or an online program. They find what's best and then invest. An investment in personal development might be through books or attending a Tony Robbins event, whatever is best for them to receive greatest return on their investment. Find what's best, and then invest.

The cool thing about pageantry is that because you are judged across multiple areas including your intelligence, communication skills, fashion sense, and social savvy, there are lots of ways to invest in pageantry. And, because of the nature of the role of a titleholder, when you invest wisely, it pays off over and over again – at appearances, future pageants, job interviews, social circles, and travel! A wise investment is something that will give you a lot in return.

Where you should invest is unique to each individual, so I'm going to share with you four steps to discover where you should invest and how to invest wisely.

Step #1 – Write Your List of Investments

Write down the things you want to improve about yourself and your pageant presentation. Maybe you want to be calmer on stage, understand your fashion style more, have the most jaw-dropping wardrobe, or walk like you have sexy giraffe legs. Maybe you want to level up your interview skills, learn how to do professional makeup, or be a current events wiz. Or maybe you want to soak up every moment of the experience so you have memories that last forever. Don't get too carried away here. You could list everything under the sun to be "perfect" but Rome wasn't built in day. Narrow it down to the top 10-15 things you are looking to gain from this pageant. Be super specific.

Step #2 – Look for Opportunities

For each area you want to grow in, research three opportunities you could invest in that would get you a high return. Take your time here. It's likely you'll first think of things that are free and/or cheap like watching a bunch of YouTube makeup tutorials and buying cheap products from CVS. If learning to do professional makeup is important to you this year, then this is not the way to go. There are better investments that will get you to your goal faster and better than you could on your own. For example, calling up a professional makeup artist and scheduling a makeup lesson. Will that cost you? Yes. Will it be a wise investment? Yes! You'll know how to do your own makeup now for every pageant, event, and appearance you ever do in the future. That's a smart investment.

Step #3 – Research

Research each item on your list and choose the best option to learn, perform, or practice what you need to in order to increase the skills on your list. Think more about the long-term payoff than the short term. Some coaches charge just $20 for a mock interview. Don't spend $100 for a series of bad mock interviews. If it's not helping you dramatically then, it's a bad investment. Instead, spend $200 on something you can walk away knowing that you did it once and did it the right way. Find what's best, and then invest.

When you invest your money wisely you'll know because it will have an impact that outlasts the immediate results. You'll make new friends, learn new things, grow in multiple areas, and best of all, you'll reach your goals. If something isn't helping you reach your goals, then it isn't even worth $1.

A wise investment is one that will yield a high return. If you waste your money on a bad investment (like a dress that isn't appropriate for the pageant system or a coach that doesn't know what they're talking about), then you will lose that money, and instead of your investment helping to create greater success, it's just gone.

Your pageant investments must be wise. Don't rely on your mom and dad to tell you whether you can or can't buy something. Instead, set a budget for yourself, decide what is important right now, research your opportunities and invest wisely.

A wise investment will allow the river to keep flowing. Find what's best, and then invest.

CHAPTER 8

STANDOUT FROM THE OTHERS

22: The Girl With the Most Energy Wins

WinAPageant.com/22

As you know, being a pageant titleholder takes a lot of energy. Often times, you have to smile and wave for three hours regardless of how cold the NYC air is on Thanksgiving Day. You may have to have entertaining conversations with media correspondents on 2.5 hours of sleep without yawning on national television. You'll likely have to speak with grace and gratitude to a school auditorium full of teenagers before lunchtime. And you'll definitely have to politely negotiate the constant pull of requests for your time and your resources.

All competitions are won in the combination of strategy and tenacity. Strategy is the process of preparation, and tenacity is the proper management of energy, especially when the tanks are under pressure. Many great leaders, including one of my favorites, Blair Singer, say, "The person with the most energy wins." Blair relates this to business, relationships, and life, but this concept also applies to pageantry.

I first heard a version of this as it relates to pageantry from Emily Wills, Miss Pennsylvania America 2006. I was competing to be her successor. It was a grueling pageant week for me, on top of the many months of difficult preparation I endured. I honestly couldn't wait for it to be over.

The night of finals, I sat next to Emily in the hair and makeup chairs and asked for one piece of advice about success at Miss America. Her response was completely unexpected. She said, "Tenacity. The winner is the one who makes it to the finish line." I wish I had asked her this question months before because the night of finals is not the time to be attempting to reserve energy.

What Emily was teaching me was that pageant winners have to know how to effectively manage their energy – first to win, and then to serve as the titleholder. Right after a winner wins, she is usually escorted to a reception where she has to give an acceptance speech, then smile for photos with everyone and their brother – literally. Then, she may be launched into a weeklong media tour followed by a professional on-location photo-shoot on the beach – hopefully not in the winter.

If you don't know how to manage your energy, you will be left exhausted even before the pageant ends, and that is how women lose pageants.

The good news is that energy is a renewable resource. If you feel low on energy, what do you do? Take a nap, eat healthy food, take a vacation, listen to uplifting music, surround yourself with encouraging people, laugh, meditate, or workout. Renewing your energy seems to come more intuitively than conserving energy.

Conserving energy is key in pageantry. The year I won Miss California, there was an outstanding contestant in my group. She looked the part to perfection, she was always at the gym when I arrived and still there when I left each day, she was constantly posting on social media, and diligent about her meals. The night before the pageant, she was on fire at the gala!

I remember looking at her all week long thinking I ought to perk it up a bit and dig into my energy reserve to match her outgoing personality that night, but that wasn't my strategy and certainly would have drained my tenacity. Instead, I stuck the course of energy conservation for the moment to shine. It's a subtle difference with a huge impact. I won and she didn't place.

So, how do you manage your energy? Glad you asked. Two ways: Maximize the things that add energy and minimize the things that drain energy. Throughout your day, you'll encounter many things that drain your energy, like decision-making (even the smallest decisions of what to have for breakfast take energy), arguing, emotional distress, physical activity, and even just being awake! The more drainage you have during the day – or pageant week, in our case – the more you need to fill up and refuel.

In pageantry, I've found that the most draining activities are:

- Ignoring a Preparation Plan (workout plan, training strategy), which leads to feelings of regret and "shoulda, coulda, woulda"
- Mindset of comparison, which makes you focus on your lack rather than your value
- Worry of not winning, and focusing on your fears
- Drama of negativity, gossip, complaining, hurting others, being mean
- Last-minute decision-making, unpreparedness
- Responsibility of activity

Here are the best ways to stop draining yourself during pageant week:

Don't self-sabotage! Stick to your plan. Trust the process and the strategy that was created for your pageant. If you put thought into how you'd win, don't sell yourself short. If you were strategizing to stop eating sweets and do cardio twice a day, then put down the donut. If you know you're supposed to have a coaching call every week, don't miss it! Self-sabotage is ridiculous and draining.

Don't care so much about what the other contestants are doing, thinking, eating, saying, or wearing. Thoroughbreds run their own race. You have a strategy, stick to it. Shield against being drained by other people's strategies during pageant week.

Don't worry about not winning. Keep your eyes on the prize. If you've done your homework, brought your best self, and prepared exceptionally, then it doesn't matter how much you worry, it will not help you. It will only drain your energy reserve. Shield yourself against the outcomes you can't control.

Don't be drug into the negative drama. The moment someone utters even a whisper of gossip or negativity, find a polite excuse and remove yourself from the situation. Words are powerful, just hearing negative comments will let them seep into your subconscious. Shield against drainage from negativity at all times.

Don't leave yourself with last minute decisions to make. Make all decisions before you go to the pageant. That goes for exactly which earrings you'll wear for the school visit and how you'll wear your hair for the trip to the zoo. Be detail-oriented in advance so you can shield against decision making during the pageant.

Don't leave all the duties up to you alone. It takes a team to win a pageant. That's why there are vendors for every element of competition from wardrobe styling to makeup and hair. Hire someone else to do what you don't have to do. You can't hire someone to walk the runway for you, but you can hire someone to do your makeup and zip your dress. Don't attempt to create a 3-month pageant training strategy on your own. Hire someone to do that for you. Your energy is precious and the more that you delegate the things other people could do (and do better than you could, by the way), the more energy you'll conserve for what you do best!

Managing your energy isn't about being a wallflower or not talking to other contestants (unless those things are particularly draining in which case I recommend limiting them), it's about being wise in where you put your efforts.

Step#1 – Make a list of the things that you know are particularly draining for you – put them in two categories, one to avoid altogether (this would be the gossip and drama-rama), and the other one for things that are necessary to pageantry (creating a winning pageant strategy, makeup, hair, platform).

Step #2 – From that list, in the category of avoidance, I want you to brainstorm a way you can avoid these. For example, the other contestants talking negatively, you could say, "excuse me" and exit the conversation. For everything on the other list of necessary pageant elements, think of a person that you can outsource those things to. I know that a pageant preparation strategy is on every pageant girls' list, and that is my specialty, so if I were you, I'd write Alycia Darby next to that one.

Step #3 – Start outsourcing. Find the contact information for someone on every element of your pageant needs. Reach out to them in advance to ensure that they are a fit. If it's a makeup artist you love, make sure they are available that day so that if not, you can find someone who is.

Step #4 – Make a list of all the things that add energy to you! For me, those things are yoga, prayer, eight hours of sleep, and a giant spinach and fruit salad. Start to do more of these things every day to put energy back into your essence.

The hardest part about this is not the outsourcing – it's avoiding the draining activities. So start practicing that now. Only spend your time with uplifting people, walk away from negative conversations, stay focused on your own strategy, and don't concern yourself with the comparison of others.

68: Avoid Becoming the Deer in Pageant Headlights

WinAPageant.com/68

Oh, the dreaded 'deer in headlights' look. I know you know what I'm talking about because you've seen someone else do it and it's so awkward for your whole audience. The poor girl usually doesn't even know it's happening until she gets the photos back. She blames the photographer for catching her at a bad moment until she gets the DVD and realizes it was hard to catch her in a good moment.

The 'deer in the headlights' phrase describes the pageant girl that walks onto stage and nearly freezes like a deer that steps out onto the road and freezes looking right at it until it's hit at full speed. It's awful. For everyone. But especially for the woman that doesn't even realize she's doing it.

First, let me explain what is going on in the woman's mind when she is standing there, looking stunningly gorgeous but with giant doe-eyes, frozen in a stiff pose and barely breathing. This happens when a woman is fully aware of her surroundings and not at all aware of her own existence. This happens from nerves. It's like an out of body experience. You end up just floating along, blacked out to what your body is doing and so focused on what everyone else is doing and thinking. When you walk off stage, you could explain exactly what you saw in the audience, the judges faces, the kid picking his nose in the front, but you have no recollection of not breathing, blinking or connecting with the audience.

Women that have little experience on a stage are more susceptible to becoming the deer in the headlights because they aren't used to understanding their body awareness under spotlights when they are being watched, not to mentioned judged. Women with excellent self awareness on stage are usually dancers, athletes, and singers – people who have performed so much they are unaffected by the dynamic change from being in the audience to be in the spotlight.

A pageant is just like any stage performance. All the people in the audience are behaving normally and the people on the stage are captivating the attention of the audience to spark an emotion that entertains and delights. It's a form of one-way communication that not everyone is skilled at. When someone who is not used to that level of responsibility and communication is brought onto a stage, she could easily freeze under the pressure.

The best way to cultivate this self-awareness is through actual stage experience. Take up a dance class where you have to perform in front of your classmates. Join Toastmasters where you practice giving speeches to the group. Or spontaneously bust out into song and dance at the mall.

Truly the best way to experience the spotlight is to jump in. But, I also have for you a less-vulnerable way to remain aware of your own actions while on stage and communicate with your audience appropriately.

Mostly, it's a mindset shift. You have to recognize that your job is to perform, that means to communicate an emotion and engage a reaction that delights your audience. To do that, you have to fully own your responsibility and know what you want to communicate. That's where my Mantra Exercise comes in. A mantra is something that you say over and over to evoke a reaction. People use mantras to stop eating junk food by saying, "I love healthy food. I love healthy food." over and over. Some people start every day with powerful mantras like, "I am wise, powerful, and influential. Today, I will conquer whatever comes my way."

I use mantras in pageant competition to evoke an emotion that I want to communicate to my judges and audience. Here's how: For every phase of competition, I consider what emotion I want to evoke in my audience and in myself. For example, in evening gown, I want to evoke a sense of love and grace. I want my audience to say, "She was so lovely and gracious." Knowing what I want them to say, I can create what I want to communicate to get that reaction. In this example, I want to communicate something like, "Thank you so much for having me. It's an honor to be here." And their response would be the feeling of love and grace.

For swimsuit, I want to evoke an emotion from my judges like, "I want to go hang out with her. She looks like she's on top of the world!" So my mantra is "I'm having a pool party. You're totally invited."

As I enter stage for each phase of competition, I say that mantra in my mind over and over and 'perform' that phrase to communicate with my audience. Every one of my clients that has done this says the same thing, "it helped me relate to my audience and I wasn't as nervous!"

There are 2 keys to creating your mantras. First, they have to be authentic to you. Something you would actually say in real life. Second, they have to include your audience in some fashion. I make sure mine say "you" somehow: "*you* are totally invited" "thank *you* for having me." That helps to make sure you are actually communicating with them and not just in la-la land on stage saying things like "I look great. I worked hard." Your performance has to communicate with the judges. Communication is key to not looking like a deer in pageant headlights.

57: Getting Into the Top 5 by Overcoming Fear of The Unknown

WinAPageant.com/57

A whopping majority of people – I'd say about 90% – are average in reaching their potential in life and in pageants. That's why it's such an honor to place in the top 5 of 50 contestants. I've coached thousands of women all across the US in every major pageant system, and the ones that end up in the top 10% are the doers, not the dreamers.

Every single woman competing in a pageant has a dream – she believes she can make it to the top. She feels alive when she envisions herself winning the title. She's passionate and excited. But only 10% of women competing (who also have the dream, by the way) are doers. Only 10% of these women take consistent and committed action toward their goal. The top five are an elite group of action-takers that will likely be successful no matter what they attempt to accomplish. Why? Partially because they aren't afraid of what they don't know.

I'm going to share with you how to overcome the fear of the unknown and create a strategy for your pageant success that will get you into the top 10% of elite pageant women.

First, let's understand the Fear of the Unknown. It could be the fear of the outcome (success or failure) or fear of the process. Fear of outcome is that they are afraid of either succeeding and having to change everything they're comfortable with or failing and having to face the fact that they need a new idea. Fear of the process is not having an actual strategy to follow step-by-step to know the path you have to take to get to the winner's circle.

These fears generally stem from three areas:

(1) Lack of experience in risk-taking
(2) Lack of education
(3) Lack of multi-dimensional identity

They lack experience in risk-taking.

Women who haven't taken risks in the past can't adequately understand the comparison of a benefit over a risk. They have a hard time seeing how overcoming a risk can bring them benefits beyond the obvious. It takes someone with experience in risk-taking to point out these benefits and train someone to recognize that they are able to pivot as more information is received. This fear from lack of experience shows up in my coaching as initial excitement followed by a series of "what if" questions:

What if it doesn't work?

What if that's not what they want?

What if I run out of time?

What if it works sooner than we planned?

What if I don't have enough?

When my clients ask these rhetorical questions, my answer is not "Oh, I never thought of that. If you run out of time you're screwed, so let's not even do it." Ha! That would never happen. Instead, I give an answer. What if you do run out of time? Well, I suppose you'll be just half way there. Whoop-de-do. What if you don't have enough for everyone? Well, you'll have to create a wait list and then make more. What if it doesn't work? Well, we'll have to analyze why and create a new plan of action. My point is that if you answer these questions and follow it down the rabbit hole, you'll discover your fears are likely irrational and you'll be much more certain about your need to take action.

Women who have studied abroad or frequently travel are great at diminishing fear of the unknown because they've had so many risky experiences where they've failed or had success, with language, cultural norms, moving to a new area and getting lost, that they realize the benefit of trying is awesome compared to the risk of failing. Risks of the unknown become less and less scary because they've been there, done that, and figured it out before. They understand that if they can overcome this challenge, the benefit will be huge.

The top 10% are focused on the benefits, not the risks.

They lack education.

Women who have not had an educational experience have a limited *understanding* of their abilities to grow and develop new skills. This isn't about ability. We all are capable of learning, but if you haven't stretched those muscles in a while, it's going to be hard to *believe* it's possible. This fear usually shows up in my coaching when someone has "I can't" and "I don't" beliefs. I can't lose weight. I can't afford it. I can't speak like that. I could never do that. I don't know how.

Women that easily overcome this are the ones that are currently pursuing education in their life in any other area: a college student, a woman who signs up for snowboarding lessons rather than sitting out the trip, a woman who follows cookbooks to learn new recipes, someone who is always watching how-to videos for everything from cleaning a coffee pot to programming a cell phone. These women know that if they can't do it now, all they have to do is find someone to teach them how.

Someone who is coachable doesn't say, "I can't." They ask questions to learn. How can I lose weight? How can I afford it? How do others speak like that? How could I do that? Can you show me how?

The top 10% are investing in their education right now.

The lack a multi-dimensional identity.

Another common reason for fears is a one-dimensional identity. If we feel our identity is all wrapped up in one area, we're less likely to take a risk that could result in failure. That's why parents are criticized when they are only telling their kid how great they are in one area rather than pointing out skills in many areas of what makes them who they are. This usually shows up as the woman that "wants to prove it to everyone that she can do it." Or she believes that this will be the solution to all of her other problems. "If I just win Miss America, everyone will love me." Not true, hunny. You need to get your credibility and self-worth from other areas of life before a pageant win can even be in the cards.

The women that are least likely to suffer from this are those that have a solid support system in their faith with God. They know their identity is in Him and their self-view is divine. Others gain support from people from areas outside of pageantry, like their husband, family, best friends, mentors, and coach who know and love them for other strengths and skills that they own as an individual. They're identity is multi-dimensional. They are a daughter, sister, wife, professional, mentor, volunteer, mother, and beauty queen.

The top 10% know they aren't defined by the outcome of the pageant.

All people have these fears – even the most successful people. The difference between the average 90% and the women standing in the top 5 at the end of the pageant is that these 10% of elite women chose coachable over comfortable. Ninety percent of people want to keep doing what they're doing so they don't have to do what they don't already know.

It's the Miss USA contestant who says, "What if I win and have to move to NYC? I've never lived in a big city before" versus the one who says, "I need to learn about living in a big city so that I'm ready for when I win and need to move there."

It's the 18-year-old Miss America contestant who says: "What if I win this year and I don't get all those years to learn how it's done and make connections?" verses the one who says, "I better buckle down and get a strategy to make up for my lack of experience."

It's the 35-year-old woman who says, "I can't be in a pageant now because all those other girls have been competing for years. I could never do that" versus the top 10% who say, "I need to learn how to compete in a pageant against all these girls that have been doing it for years."

Many women are terrified of the Top 5 on-stage question. I tell all my clients, if you want to get a crown on your head, you WILL answer an on-stage question, so stop avoiding it and start practicing! Don't lower your expectations to your level of education and experience. Raise your education to your level of your expectations.

The top 10% of contestants don't rely on their excuses. They take a risk, get educated, and use their experience to advance themselves in pageants, career, relationships, and life. They get a strategy and get into the top 5.

60: 4 Steps to Leap Out of a Pageant Rut

WinAPageant.com/60

If you've been competing for more than a few years without winning – maybe even placing lower than you have in the past – you know exactly what I mean by "a rut." It's the sensation of lacking confidence and general chutzpa for pageantry and life. Literally, a rut is like a hole or a pit that's hard to get out of. There are three specific ways I want to look at how a rut shows up for us.

First, in real life, it may show up as analysis paralysis – where you just keep rehashing the past over and over. You obsess over the judge's notes, you go crazy with too many options and you just sit there without movement until the last possible second when you have to finally choose something and you're never really happy with your choice. It's like standing still in the sand as the waves crash over your ankles and each time the ground erodes more and more from under your feet. The stronger the wave, the deeper you sink, until finally you're knocked off balance.

Secondly, a rut can show up as doing the same thing over and over but getting no new place. You keep changing your gown every year, you practice your walk over and over until your feet blister, but still haven't had a breakthrough. It's like when your car is stuck in the mud and the harder you push the gas, the deeper the car sinks. The more you push, the deeper you sink.

Thirdly, a rut can show up when you keep repeating bad habits you know you need to change. You put off decisions, you don't invest in your success, and so you end up creating a habit of only having one foot in. In the meantime all your money, efforts, and time are wasted on half-effort that never had a chance of working in the first place. Instead of doing what you know you should do, you're *always* cutting corners, *always* dodging bullets, and *always* losing when you wish you could win.

You may have heard of the phenomenon of the frog in hot water. If a frog is put into boiling water, it will immediately jump out to save itself because it immediately recognizes the danger of the situation. But if a frog is put in room temperature water, which is then slowly brought to a boil, the frog will stay in the hot water until it dies. What a way to go, man!

This is an illustration of how we sometimes manage our lives. If we're immediately dropped into a situation that's clearly bad – a relationship, an apartment, a new job, a change in the weather – we get out immediately. But when we slowly dig ourselves into a rut, it gets worse and worse. We aren't taking inventory regularly. We stay stuck until we're dead – physically, mentally, and/or emotionally.

There's only one way out of a rut and it's to leap out onto a clear path with a solid foundation. Right now, you're going to get a step-by-step process how to leap out of the rut!

Step #1 – Be Aware. Awareness is being able to objectively understand your emotions, thoughts, and actions. To do this for yourself, you have to take regular inventory. Keep a journal or a day log. A former roommate of mine was in a crappy relationship. On the days it was good, it was very good, but on the days it was bad, it was horrid. I told her to get a calendar and put a star on all the days that were great and a frown on the days that were bad. At the end of the month, see if the good outweigh the bad. She did the exercise and realized the good did not outweigh the bad. She ended the relationship proudly to reclaim her happiness.

It's extremely difficult to do these things for yourself in pageantry – it's hard to see yourself objectively. I offer DVD reviews for my clients. I watch their pageant – first I watch just them and fast-forward every other girl while I record individual feedback. Then, I watch the full pageant in context with the other women and give additional feedback. It's so hard to truly know what is going on with your walk or your vocal inflection or how you're showing up to others without someone who doesn't live in your body, think your thoughts, and make your actions. You have to have a third-party perspective.

A few weeks ago, I had a call with a woman who'd always had her mom and aunt "coaching" her. In about 10 minutes I was able to point out something she had never even been aware of, because she's never had a third-party share a true understanding of what she was representing.

Now, be careful because this kind of feedback can't come from just anybody. This process has to be done with a credible source – someone who knows what they're doing – and someone that you trust. Everyone will want to give you an opinion, so always consider the source. If it applies, modify. If not, let it fly.

Step #2 – Get a Strategy. If it was easy to get unstuck or you knew how, you'd have done it by now. It's not easy, you don't know, and you haven't gotten out. You actually have to do things differently than you're already doing in order to make a change. You've heard the saying that the definition of insanity is repeating the same action over and over while expecting different results. As a pageant woman, if you change your evening gown dress every year and practice your walking until your feet bleed, but still don't win…you need a new strategy.

You need to know what you can do that will actually move the needle in your performance. Changing your outfit or putting the other hand on your hip won't – I promise. Women waste hours and hours of precious pageant prep time on these silly things when they ought to get a strategy for getting media and appearances that will stack their success.

Step #3 – Take Fast Action to Stack Your Success. The first goal of every great superstar is to catch momentum. These greats know that as soon as you catch momentum, everything else will be easier. Lady Gaga was a songwriter for years and years before recording her own song to perform. When she hit the scene she took immediate action to ensure momentum – she created her crazy-cool brand with her wild dresses and big personality. Immediately, she was invited for interviews, her social media boomed, and she performed all over the nation for millions of people on TV and in concert. She stacked her opportunities for success, which set the stage for a long career on the early momentum. If you've seen documentaries on her success, she describes how she studied celebrities to understand how to quickly make a name for yourself. She implemented the strategy and it worked! That was over 10 years ago, and we still know who she is today because of the fast action on the strategy that led to momentum. Once you have your strategy, you have to take immediate and fast action and soon the snowball appears. The larger it gets the easier it rolls on its own.

My client, Lori, is a great example of momentum. When she first created her Legacy Project, a children's book, I insisted that she not stop until it was excellent. We were back and forth with the concept and the details and she had to seriously trust God in the outcome of this process. She did and it has multiplied into media appearances, a state title, and tons of traction for her platform. It's amazing what can happen when you follow your God-sized dream and put in the work to get momentum!

Step #4 – Start Immediately. The more time you have, the more progress you'll make. One of my pet peeves as a coach is when pageant women wait until closer to their pageant to start getting coaching. Listen, I am not a magician. If you wait until two weeks before your pageant to get coaching, then I will give you a strategy that only takes two weeks to implement. That will not be your best strategy.

Not starting immediately truly is one of the biggest things that women don't realize is killing their opportunity to win. The week before your pageant should be stress-free, not learning new strategies and stressing yourself out to recreate the wheel. If you talk to me the week before your pageant, you will be disappointed because I can't do much with you then. The same goes for women that get excited about the strategies we talk about on their coaching call and then they wait months to implement anything.

Most of my successful clients have started their coaching programs at least nine months before their pageant. Retong in South Africa started 15 months before her pageant – that's over a year! She knows Miss South Africa is a highly competitive pageant and she wants time to rise to the level of competition. Alyssa started 11 months before her pageant. Ashley did her first professional mock interview with me six months before her pageant. I was able to give her so much feedback, homework, ideas, and strategies to implement because she had the time to really grow. It is never too early to get started. The more time we have, the more feedback I can give.

If you do your mock interview a week before the pageant, I can only give you feedback that you can actually implement between now and then because it's just not enough time to develop new skills and shift habits.

Stop spinning your wheels. Please do not let the warm water around you turn into a boil. If you are in a rut – in pageantry or in life – you have got to leap out of that mess before you shrivel up and die. Become aware by getting a third-party perspective. Get a strategy that aligns with your goals. Take fast action to stack your success. Start right now!

91: 3 Steps to Turn Your Fears Into Pageant-Winning Strengths

WinAPageant.com/91

When you first sign up for a pageant, you're excited, fearless, and secure in your ability to win. As the pageant gets closer and closer, fear starts to creep in. It shows up in many ways. We're going to look at fear manifesting as the Impostor Syndrome and the Skeletons in Your Closet.

Impostor Syndrome comes from focusing on your flaws. It's when you start to believe that despite all the great things weighing in your favor, you don't belong in this place, with this title. Fear forces you to look at your lack of experience, your flaws, your insecurities, and your shortcomings to tell you that you are an impostor! You aren't a true queen.

God would tell you otherwise. He would say, "You can do all things through Christ who gives you strength."

To advance to a new level, you have to do something you've never done before. If you've done it, then it wouldn't be so impressive. If you were Miss Utah USA last year, and you're competing against the same girls this year with that year of experience, it's not fair and it's not going to help you reach any higher goals.

God wants you to do things outside of your strengths so that He will shine.

The second way that fear manifests is with what I call the Skeletons in your closet. These are all the yucky things that this world did to you that you've shoved into the back of your mind and heart – into the depths of the closet. You haven't taken the effort to clean out the closet so the skeletons are still lurking there haunting you.

The Skeletons in your closet are the things you hope no one ever knows about you: your past, your upbringing, your misfortunes, your mistakes, and your bad choices. Fear wants you to focus on the guilt, confusion, and shame of your past and uncontrollable circumstances. Fear, guilt, shame, and confusion – those things didn't come from God.

He can't give you those things because God is love! God wants to restore your joy, hope, peace, and your drive to seize what He has claimed for you!

Listen, we all have things we fear. That is the nature of the world. It's a constant battle to overcome these thoughts and rise above. And you have the responsibility to do so. I'm going to teach you three steps to fight off the Imposter Syndrome and clear out the Skeletons in your closet. This lesson is based on the Romans 8 Principle.

In the bible, Romans 8:28 says, "And we know that God causes everything to work together for the good of those who love God and are called according to his purpose for them."

I love how it says, "His purpose for them" meaning, what God wants for us. I believe that God put a dream on the inside of your heart to win this pageant. He gave you a vision to become someone great and when you achieve it you'll bring glory to Him. If this is truly His purpose for you, then He's going to work together all things for good for you. How cool is that? This exercise will strengthen your faith that even the worst things can be made good.

Step #1 – Get a piece of paper and make two columns. In the left column, make a list of all the things that you see as a disadvantage. Write each item on a new line. What disqualifies you from winning? Your short hair, your job, your small town, whatever it is that you think could be a good excuse for you to not win. This should be easy because we are trained by society to compare our shortcomings to others' best features. Still, dig deep. Consider what you hope no one will ever find out about you. What skeletons are you hiding? Do this in a private place because it's likely that these fears will carry emotions with them. Especially if they are things you haven't considered before.

For example, you may write down that you are embarrassed that you are an animal rights activist, but you ran over your cat two years ago and didn't realize until you came home to its lifeless body. That's a skeleton that fear would tell you is a disqualifier. I'm going to help you prove that it's not.

Step #2 – In the right column next to each line item, I want you to get creative and think about how this item could be used for the greater good of your family, your community, your city, your office, your school, your state, or your nation when you win this pageant. What impact will this line item have on your reign for the better? This will not be easy. I'm asking you to function outside of the norm, to turn your perspective from fear to love. This is hard for most humans, but it is wildly transformative.

Using the previous example about the cat, you may actually be able to share this story and how even a person with the best intentions could have an accident, which is why everyone needs to take necessary precautions to protect their pets.

Take your time on this step. There may be some item that you struggle to find the good. Let God reveal it to you; trust that He will handle that one. If you can create a list of reasons to choose love, how much more will God use your shortcomings to show off His strength? So much more!

Step #3 – The final step is to start believing it. To truly believe something is to act as though it is truth. Believing in something is more than just knowing it exists, it's behaving and living as though it is the highest truth. If you ran over your cat and you can use that story for a greater good, start doing it now.

God promises that He causes ALL things (even the things you think are ugly, even the things you're embarrassed by, even the things you wish weren't true) to work together for the good of those who love Him and are called according to His purpose for them.

Don't let fear bully you into losing your pageant. Look it in the face and scream Romans 8:28 at it: "God causes everything to work together for the good of those who love God."

93: Your Pageants Worst-Case Scenario

WinAPageant.com/93

When things get tough in pageantry (or in life), sometimes we jump to the worst-case scenario. We get overwhelmed and terrified by the worst possible thing that could go wrong, and then we obsess over it until we can't possibly imagine any other way except the worst way. We somehow end up pushed against the wall so much that we want to just turn our back on the whole situation and fly off the ledge into what we know is sure disaster and self-sabotage. It almost seems better than this worst-case scenario. Ever been there? Clearly, I'm speaking from experience.

My first encounter with "the ledge" was in my second pageant. The first pageant I did I had no chance of winning and I didn't really care to win, I was just doing it for fun. But my second pageant was a local preliminary title that would qualify me to compete at the state pageant in the Miss America system. It also happened to come with a big chunk of scholarship gold and it took place in my home community in a grandstand that could seat over 2,000 people. There were 2 weeks of daily rehearsals before the pageant day. I signed up for the pageant because I wanted to dance in front of the huge audience, which I hadn't done in my 20 years of life. I definitely didn't want to win. I just wanted to dance.

The first week of rehearsals was fun – we learned the opening number dance, practiced our talents, learned the walking patterns, did some mock interviews, and met the other girls who were all awesome. We knew rehearsals would get more intense the next week since the pageant was getting closer. At the end of week one, I started thinking that I may actually be in the running for this title. I had a really great talent and was the only person really enjoying the interviews. That weekend, I forgot all about it and just kept practicing my dance over and over.

When we came back on Monday for rehearsal, I started paying more attention. I discovered I could potentially be in the top three.

That night, I called my sister, Amy. She's older than me and she's an engineer, so she was my go-to for solid, logical advice. She always knows what to say and how to say it – even today as adults.

I explained to her how I just wanted to dance and now I'm looking around and thinking I may accidently win this thing. I needed her advice on how I was going to get out of it. Should I quit or should I just do badly for the rest of the pageant so I didn't win?

I was officially on the ledge. I was asking how to quit. I wasn't asking for help through the fog, I was looking to get out of it the fastest, easiest way possible. I wanted to give up completely.

Maybe you've been here before, in pageantry or in life – where you have an internal battle between jumping into a pit so you don't have to face the looming future you didn't plan for, or turning around, walking into the room with your head held high and facing the music (which always seems much harder).

Now I have the wisdom of knowing that God has plans for me (and for you). In Jeremiah 29:11, God declares, "For I know the plans I have for you. Plans to prosper you and not harm you, plans to give you hope and a future."

When I was on the phone with my sister that night, I was scared. I didn't want a future in pageantry because I didn't know what I was doing. It was my first time competing, and because they always said you had to compete a few times before winning, I felt that if I won everyone, was going to be mad at me and the whole community would see me as a fraud. Plus, I was such a tomboy I didn't really even like wearing heels and now I had to pretend I loved them if I won. And how would I be able to balance everything with college and all I was involved in, and did I really even want to give energy to a full year of service when I was going to be turning 21 soon?

I rattled all this off to Amy with panic so she would empathize. I expected her to jump in the circus of fear I'd built and play along with negative comments and support of me quitting. I'm so glad she didn't jump in, but rather shared a message of hope.

I still remember her response. It had very little emotion and was overly matter-of-fact. She simply said, "Oh, just have fun with it. If you win, you can always give the crown back. People do that all the time."

People actually don't do that all the time, but I didn't know that and neither did she. Her advice was enough to remove my fear completely. This massive, grotesque, dark beast of fear I'd created was gone in a flash. It was so small and flippant now. I thought, "She's right. If it's so bad, I'll just give it up."

In an instant, she talked me off the ledge. Amy showed me another possible ending to the story, one that didn't include all my built-up fear. One that was more hopeful and brighter than the hideous worst-case scenario I'd thought up. After all, the worst thing that could happen was I'd win, and then I'd just smile, remove the crown from my head, and say to the first runner up, "Oh, here you go, sweetie." (Knowing what I know now makes this story extra hilarious.)

Today is your day to get down from the ledge and find hope in your situation. We're clearing the fog, sister! We're going to take a calculated, logical approach. We're releasing the emotion and looking at the facts.

Step #1 – Brainstorm all the worst-case scenarios. This one should be easy. This is the fog in your face that you're stuck in now. It's a big, hairy, scary "what-ifs" you've been building up in your head for days, weeks, maybe even years. I find it easier to write them by starting with "The worst thing that can happen is…" Don't waste your time thinking up ridiculous worst-case scenarios. Instead, look at what already has you frozen in fear. Don't be silly and say, "I'll fall and my pinky finger will go into a judge's eye and they'll go blind…" I want you to dig up real, actual fears that could be keeping you from being your best self.

For example:
The worst thing that can happen is…I'll win.
The worst thing that can happen is…I'll lose.
The worst thing that can happen is…I'll trip on stage.

The worst thing that can happen is…I'll blank out during my interview. The worst thing that can happen is…I'll be made fun of for a few weeks.

You get the idea.

Step #2 – Find a solution. For every single line item that you believe is the worst-case scenario, I want you to come up with how you would realistically handle this if it really did happen to you. If you fell on stage, what would you actually do? Run off stage crying? No. You'd get up, smile, maybe laugh a bit and keep walking. If you blanked out during your interview, would you stand there for an hour until someone brought you a glass of water? No. You'd say something like, "I'm sorry, I'm really nervous." Then you'd think of an answer or say, "Could you ask me something else?"

See what I mean? We're preparing for the worst-case scenario before it even happens. Go through all of your worst-case scenarios and create a solution.

Step #3 – Are you willing? Now, the third step is vital to this whole thing. Step 3 asks, "Am I willing to go for it anyway?" This is like asking yourself if you are willing to risk this worst-case scenario for the opportunity to compete. Are you willing to risk the worst-case scenario for the hope of your future?

For example, if the worst thing that can happen to you is that you could lose and that cute boy you like won't ask you to the dance so you'll have to go with your girlfriends, that's probably not a good enough reason to quit. You're likely willing to risk the lost dance date.

If the worst thing that can happen is your final answer will become a viral video and you'll have to turn it into a Hollywood hosting career, you're probably willing to risk it.

If the worst thing that can happen is your sick grandmother will pass away while you're on stage and you haven't seen her in 10 years, you may decide it's not worth the risk. This would be a great reason to quit the pageant.

When my sister said I could give the crown back if, in the worst-case scenario, I actually won, it seemed totally reasonable to me. So much that in that moment, I believe that if I did win I'd just give up the crown that night. I was willing to risk that. Of course, I'm not suggesting that truly be your way out. But from my young, immature perspective, it made sense at the time.

Read your full list back to yourself. Be honest – are you willing to risk the worst-case scenario or is it wise to respectfully bow out now?

The irony of my pageant story is that shortly after my sister talked me into sticking with it, I decided I actually wanted to win. My mindset completely turned around (I believe now that God had this in my path and He didn't want me to miss out on it). I won the pageant. I was given over $4,000 in scholarship dollars, placed in the top ten at the state pageant, impacted my entire community in a major way, met some of the most amazing leaders and mentors I've known, and started a 10-year pageant career that led to a full-time coaching business. I have been blessed in order to be a blessing to others.

God knows what He's doing. Don't let fear be the thing that holds you back from your win. Make your list of worst case scenarios and discover how you'll overcome them so nothing can hold you back from what God has in store for you!

78: 3 Steps to Become *Willing* to Win Your Pageant

WinAPageant.com/78

A few weeks ago I was watching my church's sermon on live stream. The pastor started by holding up a $20 and inviting anyone to come get it. A few people stood up. But with a whopping 500 people at the service, why didn't 500 people stand up?

They thought someone else would get there before them and their efforts would be wasted. They thought they'd look greedy, rude, or poor and didn't want to be judged. They thought it was a joke and maybe he wouldn't give it away after all and then they'd feel stupid for running up. It was more trouble to get out of their seat than to receive the value of a $20.

Everyone was invited to come get the money, but only a few people moved, and ONE of those people was $20 richer that night. His sermon talked about how God wants to give us stuff, but people are too lazy to go get it.

There's a difference between ability to have what we want and willingness to go and get it. Ability is having access to the resources to achieve what is great. Willing is the desire to take action in one direction by leaving the comfort of another. For example, you may be able to walk. That doesn't mean you're never going to sit, but you are able to walk if you are willing. Willingness is standing up from your comfortable couch and walking.

It's like this. Let's say you're watching a great TV show. It's late and you're thirsty and tired and enjoying the show so much you don't want to get up for a cup of water. You're able to go quench your thirst, but you aren't willing to leave the comfort of your couch to do so. You just want someone else to bring you a cup or a magical fairy to make you no longer thirsty. This is how some people live their whole lives — waiting around for opportunities to come to them rather than reaching out and taking them.

It's not complex, but it's not easy. "If it were easy, everyone would be doing it." I'm going to break goal achievement down into a simple process. Doing the work is going to be the hardest part.

Step #1 – List your goal.

Step #2 – List the top three things in the way of your goal that you can control (what makes you unable).

Step #3 – Ask yourself if you are willing to change what you need to in order to get what you want. If not, then find a new goal. If yes, then make an action plan to get where you want to go!

For example, let's say your goal is to lose weight. The three things in your way might be your love of food, sugar cravings, and not having a gym nearby. Are you able to change this? Yes. Are you willing to give up sugar, change your food habits, and work out from home?

If your goal is to get a job that pays $100,000, the things standing in your way may be your current education, your location in a small town, and your limited network. Are you able to change these things? Yes. Are you willing to move, go back to school, and meet the right people?

Your goal may be to win your pageant and the three things in the way are you don't know what to change, you don't have enough money for wardrobe, and you don't know what type of platform to choose. Are you able to improve these things? Yes. Are you willing to save your money, get a coach, and be open to starting a new direction?

Now it's your turn – go write down the things in the way of your goals. Ask yourself if you are willing to overcome these. It's less about being able to change and more about being willing. If you're willing, start immediately.

59: Making Pageants Important Enough to Win

WinAPageant.com/59

There's no doubt that if your 5-year-old son woke up with a fever and bumps all over his arms, you'd cancel work meetings, tell them you're not coming, and demand to get an appointment with the pediatrician. But if he woke up healthy but cranky, you'd tell him, "Hunny, Mommy loves you. Now, put on your shoes; you're going to school today."

If your best friend suggested you order pizza with olives and you hate olives, you'd whine until she agreed to order it half-with and half-without, but if the guy you liked made the exact same suggestion, you may just shut your mouth and choke them down!

If your doctor tells you to lose 30 pounds or be dead in a year, you'll join a gym, hire the most expensive trainer, and start drinking shakes for breakfast. But eating salads for dinner and skipping your nightly glass of wine after a long day to lose five pounds for your friend's wedding is not so easy.

The only difference in each of these scenarios is the level of importance placed on the intended outcome. If the outcome is important like healing your child, impressing your crush, or saving your life, our natural survival instincts kick in and immediate and impressive action is required to ensure your success. So, why is it that women don't take impressive action to win pageants? Because it's not seen as important.

First, the culture of our world paints pageantry as an unimportant hobby, something that only silly blonde girls do to play dress up and pretend to be a princess. This image is obviously erroneous to those of us who have put in the work to climb the ladder of impact and success. But it certainly shapes the minds of women at the starting line.

Second, when the hard work happens behind the scenes, all that's seen is the performance, and, of course, a true professional makes their work look easy and effortless. When you see this, it's easy to fool yourself into believing that it is in fact easy and effortless. It's like when you watch a famous A-list actor write, perform, and produce several movies in one year; or a professional model on the cover of a magazine – they make it look so easy, you think "I could do that."

Third, when we don't know what true gold lies at the end of the rainbow, it's hard to start the climb up the rainbow. If something is not important, it's easy to just sit back and keep peacefully dreaming. When we know the value and importance of something, it immediately moves to the top of our list of priorities.

Everything that's important has a strategy and an investment of time, money, and energy – everything!

For example, even the basic daily task of picking out your clothes for the day. You don't need a strategy for that, unless you're giving a big presentation at work that could land you a promotion. Or you sit next to your crush in your Tuesday-Thursday 8am speech class. Or you want to go straight to work after you leave the gym and need to take everything with you.

These situations make choosing an outfit very important, and you have a strategy; you're willing to invest in something of quality, and you take the time to make it happen.

There are lots of women that compete in pageants, but most women – 90% – don't see it as important enough to have a strategy and invest the time, money, and effort in order to win. They believe it's either silly to even try, ought to be easy, or not worth their investment. When you can identify where you stand, you'll know what's holding you back from your success.

When I first started competing, I was under the belief that only the most naturally talented, beautiful woman would win. And I thought I was that natural beauty, maybe, so it was worth a shot. I didn't really do much work, so it didn't work and I didn't win.

Once I realized that people did put in effort, I assumed it was worth the effort, so I started working on things I thought were similar to what others were working on. I still didn't think I needed an Olympic strategy with weekly training to get to the top until I competed in my first national pageant and realized that everyone else had an Olympic strategy and weekly training.

That's when I started to fully go all in! I got the strategy, I paid for the coaching, and I put in the work, and knew exactly the real prize I was after. I see these three things come up in my clients all the time. These are deep-seeded beliefs that must be uprooted and replaced with powerful, specific actions in a strategy for success.

As a side note, it's okay if pageants aren't a priority in your life. For example, if you're having a baby, moving across country to a new job, battling a life-threatening illness, or a host of other reasons, these things are more important than a pageant at the current moment. But if winning your pageant is important to you, you'll need a strategy to get you to the top!

58: Stop Procrastinating and Start Winning

WinAPageant.com/58

Procrastination is an ever-destructive, yet temporarily pacifying act; it's a phenomenon that slowly chips away at your self-esteem, efficiency, and progress and ultimately sabotages your success. Procrastination is defined as the avoidance of doing a task, which needs to be done, usually by doing more pleasurable or less urgent tasks thus putting off important tasks to a later time.

It's going biking with your friends instead of writing your essay. It's watching Netflix all day Saturday because you have so many things to do this weekend you don't even know where to start. It's checking off a bunch of simple, fun tasks that lead to nowhere because you don't know which direction to take that may lead you somewhere. Sound familiar?

I'm not saying there's not time for biking with friends and watching your favorite shows. Activities like these are certainly worthwhile, after you've accomplished what *needs* to be done.

Procrastination is caused by several things including pure laziness, low self-esteem, overwhelm, lack of clear direction, or an undefined vision of the end result.

Motivation, self-esteem, clear direction, and vision are all linked together. In pageantry, or any other quest for massive success, this is called a Strategy. When you have a strategy of how to get to where you're going, your focus is not distracted – it's laser-sharp because you see the ultimate vision and it makes you salivate for success!

I will just tell you right now: no high-level pageant titleholder is a procrastinator. Every high-level pageant contestant has a clear strategy to move them toward an ultimate vision. And the judges know that if someone is going to be crowned Miss Teen USA or Mrs. America or Miss World, then she better not be a procrastinator. Because at this level, just 10 minutes of putting something off can lead to lost opportunities and diminished success. Even the most successful women in pageantry recognize the pull toward procrastination, but they don't give in.

Bryan Tracy, a famous motivational speaker, wrote an exceptional book on this topic called "Eat That Frog! 21 Ways to Stop Procrastinating." It's a quick and easy read and gives so many practical tips to overcome this awful habit. His basic message is that if you woke up every morning and the first thing you did was eat a frog, the rest of the day would be easy! Bryan Tracy says that the first thing you do every day should be the "frog" of your to-do list - the biggest, scariest, most awful thing! Accomplishing this first will give you momentum and energy in the day. For the people who don't just wake up and eat the frog, they go all day with it hanging over their heads, draining them, and making them feel guilty for not doing it yet.

I know that you don't like procrastination. None of us do. It's a huge energy leak that makes us make other bad decisions, feel guilty, and procrastinate more. The truth is that it takes a lot of energy to eat a nasty frog, so you can't afford to lose energy by procrastinating. Bryan Tracy says, "If you have to eat a frog at all, it doesn't pay to sit and look at it for very long."

Haven't you noticed that those women who take action and get things done are the ones that are getting the promotions, always looking put together, immediately lost the baby weight, are constantly bouncing around all happy, smiling at strangers, and winning pageants? Don't they appear to be oh-so-perfect? That's because they stop energy leaks instead of let them continue to drag them down.

I also know that you sometimes tell yourself that you work well under pressure. The truth is that any task expands to take up the length of time in which it is allowed. If you have two months to turn in your pageant paperwork, you'll still turn it in the day before. If you only allow yourself 72 hours, it will magically be done in 72 hours. If you sign up late and only have 24 hours, guess what, you'll still get it done on time.

The problem for procrastinators is they spend weeks procrastinating which causes a major energy leak and brings guilt, low self-esteem, distraction, mismanagement of time, lack of decisiveness, and a host of other negative stuff. The energy leaks that hide in the corners of your life are undone tasks.

The key to stopping the energy leaks and quickly jumping into the Top 10% ---- Eat That Frog! By eating the biggest, ugliest frog first thing each morning, you'll achieve more in one week than most women will achieve all year. Of course, I broke this down into some manageable steps that I use whenever I feel low energy and need to pull myself together.

Step #1 – Make a list of all the things on your to-do list. Whatever is on your list, like calling your grandma and stopping by the store to get toilet paper, write it down.

Step #2 – Scratch off all the things you actually don't need to do. Feeling guilty or wasting time on things you don't need to do is a huge energy leak. You aren't going to sell that VCR player from the 90's…take it to the thrift store and call it a day. Leak: Stopped.

Step #3 – Circle the things that take less than 30 minutes and will immediately solve a problem. Order toilet paper on Amazon. Quit picking up a 4-pack at CVS after work every Tuesday. Get on Amazon and get a giant pack delivered to your door in two days. Done. Leak: Stopped.

Step #4 – Group what's left into frogs of similar size and texture. Put the biggest, ugliest, smelliest frogs at the top. Put the small, cute little froggies at the bottom. Warning: do not spend more than three minutes on this or it will drain even more of your energy.

Step #5 – Create a calendar to eat one of the big, ugly frogs per day until they're all done. When you wake up, look at your list and choose the biggest, ugliest, nastiest frog and eat it! Then, go about your day. By eating the frog, I mean doing the task. These frogs could be as common as going to the gym, or as unique as asking your husband to join you for couple's therapy. These are the big, nasty frogs that get put off and things only get worse.

I want to share a story of my client, Candice, who completed my coaching program, got a platform sponsor, and won her national pageant five weeks after we met. Candice is in the Top 10% – she made fast decisions, took action immediately, and boy did it pay off!

Jolie, Miss Taiwan, is another amazing Top 10% woman who took action before her pageant. She started a YouTube channel and even bought all the professional equipment to make it amazing.

Lori, who started working with me six months before her pageant, has now published a children's book that's taking off like wild fire!

Emaleigh, an 18-year-old Top 10%-er, is finishing her senior year of high school as Valedictorian, captain of her softball team, class president, and published author! She's also been eating frogs daily for six months, and she has so many more goals she'll accomplish before her pageant this summer.

Every single one of these women started with a strategy call with me where they realized that in order to achieve their big dreams, they had to have a strategy that would give them the motivation to get to the finish line of their ultimate vision.

I always say, "Motivation is the combination of understanding the process and believing in the possibility."

You can have this too. I know you have a dream in your heart, you wouldn't be reading this if you didn't believe you have something incredible that needs to be channeled toward success. You are not lazy. You're an overcomer. You have exactly what it takes to get you to your dream – that's why God put that dream inside of you: so you'd chase it. All you need is a clear strategy to understand the steps to get you to your goal and the willingness to eat big frogs every day. Do not let procrastination get in your way of success.

85: The Truth About "Fake it 'til you Make it"

WinAPageant.com/85

You've likely heard the phrase "fake it 'til you make it" before when someone is trying to beef up their confidence toward an effort they aren't prepared for. Many pageant women think "fake it 'til you make it" means to keep pretending you know what you're doing until someone gives you a big break. As if you could fake it over and over again and at some point someone will throw you a bone. Those girls never actually make it. The people that have succeeded with this concept are the ones who have found the right tools and put in the work to make it.

Many people have succeeded in their careers by confidently claiming their knowledge, skills, or position before stepping into it. The difference between those that actually "make it" really depends on who stops at the "fake it" part and who moves into the "make it" phase. You fake it, and then you make it. Making it is a learning process. It's the phase of gathering information, trying new things, and growing your knowledge base until you no longer have to fake it because you've made it a part of who you are. We're all faking it as we're learning. The learning is the making process.

You have to actively participate in the making it part, not just the faking it part. Gary Cohn is a great example of this. Many years ago, he shared a cab with a financial big wig who was starting a new branch of finance in his company. Gary claimed he knew all about the topic and was hired on the spot to start two weeks later. The truth is, he knew nothing at that moment, but he knew he could figure it out! In those two weeks he bought the only book he needed that walked him through every element of the topic until he knew more than anyone else. Now, Gary is the President of Goldman Sachs, the financial giant worth almost 40 billion dollars. He faked it and then he made it.

When I coach my clients, I tell them what the pageant expects. I help them to uncover their personal truth, and then we blend that together, sometimes for the first time ever. My clients are wearing wardrobes they never would've considered, going from mascara and ChapStick to full-face highlights and bronzer, and starting to walk taller than ever. They speak with new confidence and realize their core values deeper than before.

Ann Smarty is now an SEO expert in the online world. She started by buying a website called SEO Smarty and charging low rates for web services to gain a lot of clients she could learn from. For every client, she took a deep-dive into exactly what they needed and learned everything she could on the topic until she was an expert. Then she raised her rates and is now serving businesses around the world.

The learning process is a transformation process from knowing nothing (or very little) to becoming a master. In pageantry, it's making *you* into a titleholder. For the first little while, you'll be faking it with the new wardrobe, posture, confident expression, and clear communication. But soon you'll have made it a part of who you are.

Step #1 – Determine your "it" – what is it that you need to master.
Step #2 – Find the best training tool to minimize time and maximize results so you aren't faking it for a long time.
Step #3 – Make it happen! Learn until it becomes a part of you.

Fake it until you make it a reality.

CHAPTER 9

PREPARE FOR PAGEANT WEEK

45: Being the 'It' Girl at Orientation

WinAPageant.com/45

Orientation is a sea of judgment. It's exciting and equally nerve wracking; all the would-be titleholders showing up with their best foot forward to prove themselves as the winner. I'll teach you how to show up to your orientation as the actual winner. I want my girls mistaken for the reigning titleholder because this is the first impression you'll give to the pageant director and to the other girls. You want to be sure it is accurate, inviting, and respectable.

The best way I know to prepare a girl for orientation is to use what I call the "Next Year" test. It's simple. Imagine if you were to win, next year you'll have to attend the orientation for the incoming competition class. I want you to imagine how you will be then, and adopt that persona now. The impression you leave on others is based on how you are perceived – from your look to how you make others feel. Here, I make it easy for you to recall the four specific areas of a first impression.

Area #1 – First is your picture.

You've seen some girls go to pageant orientations looking totally crazy! I know; I've seen them too. They want to "stand out" so they wear florescent pink or do some crazy hair-do. If someone took a picture of you right now, wherever you are and handed it to someone, how would that person describe you? Do you look energetic, happy, tired, proud, thoughtful, crazy? These adjectives are used based on how a person is dressed, your posture, your makeup, hair, and accessories. How do you want to be seen at orientation? Next year, when you're giving up your title, what will you wear? This year, wear that! This is who you most want to be, so be her starting now.

Area #2 –The second area to consider is your moving picture: your video.

If someone filmed you, without sound, how would you be described? Silly, bratty, shy, generous, outgoing, annoying, fun, attention seeking, secretive, scared? Next year, when you give up your title, how do you want to be seen? As the titleholder, you'll likely be buzzing around humbly answering questions, graciously meeting the other girls and building up their confidence, participating with enthusiasm in the corny icebreakers, smiling a lot, and giving credit where credit is due. So this year, do that!

Area #3 – The third consideration is your audio.

If someone recorded just 30 seconds of you talking today, how would you come off? Confident, confused, empowering, shy, mean, grateful, kind? At pageant orientation, just like in media interviews and on-stage questions, you only have a short amount of time to make a powerful and positive impression. To do that, you have to be clear about what you're after and who you are. Speak in sound bites; don't over-talk a subject. All my clients are trained on their personal brands and platforms so that no matter the topic, they are able to communicate their essence. Next year, after a year of practicing your message, you'll have this down so well that you'll be naturally doing it at orientation. But, to win, you have to do that this year. Got it?

Area #4 – The fourth area you need to be aware of is your presence.

This is the actual feeling others get just by being in the same room as you. If you walked into a room full of strangers right now, how would your energy feel to those around you? Would they describe you as illuminating, passionate, overwhelming, negative, or captivating? What feeling do you want to give others next year when you give up your title? How will people feel when you are introduced on stage as the titleholder? That's the energy you want to bring now.

Now that you're fully aware of yourself and how others view you, I have a little challenge for you. I want you to choose one day within the next week to be your day as the future titleholder. No matter what you have to do that day, whether it's going to the gym, the office, Biology class, picking up dry cleaning, shoe shopping – whatever it is, I want you to spend the whole day being the exact person you want to be as the titleholder – all day! As the winner, what will your day look like? How will you interact with others on the street? How will you treat your server, your boss, or your friends? Do this and see how well it fits. You'll know that you are fully ready to win the pageant when you can be this person in full congruence every single day – with or without a crown.

44: How to Dress like a True Pageant Queen

WinAPageant.com/44

Dressing like a true pageant queen is simple, but not so easy. It comes down to what you have in your closet. And you need to update your closet. Yes, you. I'm talking to you – the woman who's had the same hair-do for the past seven years and who is still wearing her favorite shirt from college. I'm also talking to myself here because it's high time I get a new "favorite shirt" so I don't end up in People Magazine with a side-by-side photo in the same shirt – one dated 2009 and the other 2016 like Princess Kate. If you can relate, it's time for an upgrade.

As you grow, your priorities, responsibilities, and personality change. Whether you like it or not, you're judged by your appearance, and every woman knows that what you wear has a lot to do with how you feel. If you are still holding onto things that no longer represent the new you (or the best you), then you are doing yourself a disservice, and others will know it.

At the start of each new year, I review my closet for a wardrobe update. I did this for the first time when I moved to LA several years ago because I discovered that my wardrobe was mostly built for the east coast cold where even in the summer, the buildings are freezing due to the cranked air conditioning. Plus, I needed to make some room in my closet for my newly adopted casual west coast style.

A wardrobe change was also inevitable when I stopped teaching on college campuses and started managing fitness studios. That's when I got to ditch a lot of my slacks and button ups and move into the more preferred Lulu leggings and tanks.

I actually really love the annual wardrobe revamp process because it lets me take a fresh look at who I am and how I want to present that to others. And it doesn't need to be difficult. I broke my process into seven steps.

Step #1 – Discover who you are today.

What are the three biggest roles you play in life? Do you spend eight hours a day at the office, then workout for an hour and go to play dates with the kids on the weekends? Do you go to class during the day, sorority meetings in the evenings, and volunteer on the weekends? I know you do more than just three things, but for now, just pick the top three. For me, it's working from home, working out, and going to social events. So the three main places I find myself are at home, at the gym or studio, and attending speaking/coaching/networking events.

Step #2 – Determine how you want to be at each of these things.

Do you want to be professional, comfortable, trendy, risqué? I usual want to be comfortable at home, trendy when working out, and casually fashionable at social events. Write down three words that you want to be described as at these events. My words are respectable, approachable, and fit.

Step #3 – Choose three colors you know you look absolutely great in.

These colors usually go together well because you're likely already wearing them. Some combinations to consider may include red, navy, and white OR green, white and yellow OR orange, blue and black. Mine are fuchsia, blue, and orange – though, I promise I don't regularly wear fuchsia and orange together.

Step #4 – Put a notepad and pen next to your dresser or closet.

For one full week, write down all the things you wish you had. Do you wish you had a cute blazer to throw on top of a particular outfit or a statement necklace or beige wedge sandals? Write it all down.

Step #5 – Inventory your closet (and your jewelry, accessories, nail polish, and shoes).

Pull out every single thing and ask yourself if you wore this to one of those three places, playing one of those three roles, and if you would be described as one of those three words. If not, put it in the "no" pile. If so, put it in the "yes" pile. Don't have a "maybe" pile. Your closet is the "maybe" pile and you aren't putting anything back in there unless you feel like a million bucks in it! Hanging onto "maybe" pieces isn't a part of this process. Time to make a decision. I promise, I'm helping you.

Step #6 – Fill in the blanks.

Set a specific budget and shop for the things you *need*. This is not a shopping spree for the things you want. This is just to fill in your missing pieces. What I mean is, I don't want you going out and buying six more shirts for $20 dollars each that are going to just get ratty like the last ones. Nor do I want you buying a pair of Louboutin stilettos just because you want them, but you have nowhere to wear them. Be mindful about what you're buying. Choose pieces that represent the new you and will go well with what you already have. For some of us in some stages of life, this is a major overhaul. That's how it was for me when I moved to Los Angeles and again when I quit working at universities. I basically needed a whole new wardrobe!

Step #7 – Get rid of the "no" pile.

You have a few choices of what to do with the "no" pile. You could put them in the garbage if they simply aren't usable (like bras with the underwire popping out). You could donate what you know is outdated, but still in good shape. Take it to a Good Will, Salvation Army, or Dress for Success. Or throw a clothing swap party with your girlfriends. Ask everyone to bring over their wearable "no" pile and trade clothes with your besties. Whatever you do, don't put it back in your closet.

You don't have to go through this process every year, though that would be in your best interest. I recommend at least every three years while you're still in your 20's and 30's. There's a big difference between 28 and 31. By maintaining an updated look, you'll always be seen as relevant, relatable, and forward-thinking – great qualities of a titleholder!

37: How to Choose Your Pageant Evening Gown

WinAPageant.com/37

An evening gown is one of the favorite portions of pageantry for many audience members. What you choose to wear for your crowning moment is as important as what you'd wear to accept a Grammy. I'm going to share with you key tips about where to shop, how to prepare for shopping, and what to bring to your gown appointment to find that winning pageant evening gown.

Where to Shop for Gown:
- Find a boutique with experience, like a sponsor of a pageant or someone that is engaged in the industry all over the country/world.
- Make an appointment and arrive on time.

How to Prepare to Shop:
- Arrive with energy so you can make the most of your experience and make quick decisions.
- Don't wear body makeup like fake tanner or tattoo foundation.
- Have your hair and makeup looking stage-ready.
- Have a few gown styles in mind, but keep an open mind for other styles too.
- Share your price range with your shopping assistant so they can help you search for options.
- Bring a scarf or makeup shield to use while you're trying on.
- Don't try on a gown that is far out of your budget or else you'll be disappointed when you can't afford it.

What to Bring to Your Appointment:
- Shoes you plan to wear with the gown, or similar ones

- Extra jewelry such as AB crystal and rhinestone earrings to try with your gown options
- Foam boob inserts
- Nude undergarments like Spanx
- Strapless Bra
- Decision makers like parents, director, sponsors, coach

What Determines the Price of the Gown:
- Famous Pageant Gown Designers
- Beads, crystals, jewels
- Custom designs
- Alterations

How to Respect the Store Owners:
- Touch gowns by the hanger, not the fabric
- Don't go over your appointment time
- Hang your dresses in the dressing room
- Stay positive, honest, respectful and gracious to those helping you
- Take a photo with the gown in the garment bag and post a "Thank you" on social media

83: What to Wear to Pageant Rehearsal

WinAPageant.com/83

Wardrobe is always worth considering. It's a contestant's worst nightmare to arrive to the first pageant rehearsal in sneakers and an oversized t-shirt you wore to the gym in college only to find all the other girls dressed in their Sunday best – even though the paperwork said to dress comfortably. "Comfortable" is a relative adjective. To pageant girls, it means to skip the Jessica Simpson shoes for their Michael Kors wedges and exchange rhinestones and lace for spandex and silk.

In a competition, you have to be your best all the way around. You have to exude excellence from the very beginning – that means planning your wardrobe so it's up to snuff with the competition.

You'll want to select all of your rehearsal outfits in advance and pack them according to the day you'll wear them. I recommend having your outfits start off more subdued and then save the dressier ones for closer to the pageant day. It does two things: 1) usually you'll be doing more movement in the earlier days like learning the dance and other activities so you'll want to be more comfortable, and 2) as you get closer to the title, you'll want to step up your game and feel more like a queen.

Also, consider the branding of the pageant itself. Miss International and Galaxy pageants are very glitzy and high-glamour; think rhinestones galore. The Miss USA pageant is high-fashion model-type, so less rhinestones and more sleek appeal. The Miss America system is somewhat more conservative than others but still stylish and high-class. The trick here is to envision you've already won. What would you wear if you already won the title you are competing for?

I want to break down three easy steps that will take you about 60 seconds to consider and help you plan your wardrobe for a week or more of pageant rehearsals.

Step #1 – Name your style.

I call my style "professionally fit." Most days of the week, I'm rocking Lululemon leggings and a brightly colored blouse. When I go shopping, I have a vision in my head, maybe even a Pinterest board on my phone to consider whether what I'm about to try on or buy fits my style. If not, I skip it. If it does, move on to Step #2.

Step #2 – Consider the context.

Of course, you'll consider the context being the fact that you are competing in a beauty pageant, so you can't win if you're wearing loafers and a ripped t-shirt. So, there's that. But what I mean here is to consider what you'll be doing in rehearsal on each day. If you're learning the opening number dance that day, you'll want to wear something more moveable. If you'll be in the freezing cold auditorium from 7am to 7pm, wear lots of layers.

Step #3 – Make it cover-ready.

This is the final step. You're in the dressing room fully clothed in your new potential outfit. I want you to consider this: if someone took your picture and posted it on the front of your favorite magazine, would you approve? Always wear something that you'd approve of in photos because you will be photographed and you will regret flats, pants that are a size too big, and a pilling sweater. (You'll also regret looking like Holiday Barbie at a pizza joint.)

Most rehearsals request that contestants wear snappy casual clothes. Snappy casual is something you'd wear on a first date or on a night out with the girls – usually jeans, trendy top, and fashionable accessories. Some pageants, like the Miss International Pageant have a culture of glitz and glam even in the rehearsals. Since there is no talent portion of that pageant, it's easier for contestants to wear a cocktail dress to rehearsal – and many of them do.

Great outfits to consider for any pageant rehearsal are jumpsuits, rompers, or sheath dresses – they are classy, trendy, easy to dress up, and comfortable for all day sitting, standing, and dancing. What you wear will largely impact how you feel and, ultimately, how you perform on stage that week. So, get yourself together, dress it up, and step into your future title. Don't overthink it, of course, but don't forget it either.

64: 15 Must-Have Pageant Products

WinAPageant.com/64

There are certain products that every pageant woman must have in her pageant suitcase. I put together a list of the 15 most common must-have products. Most of these products are a one-time purchase; you'll buy just once and use over and over again. You can buy them all on Amazon for less than $200 total and you'd be set for a full year of appearances and competitions. These are also great to add to your birthday, Christmas, or send-off party wish list. You can download the full list of these products with links to purchase them on Amazon in the Beauty, Truth and Grace Guidebook at: WinAPageant.com/Guide.

Beauty & Personal Care

Self-Tanner – This is an easy-to-apply lotion with a bronzer so you can see where it's been applied. For competition, I usually applied it the night before I left for orientation, slept in it, then showered off in the morning and applied again toward the end of the week as a second layer. Always test your tanner two months before your pageant so you can tell how it goes on and how even it stays on your body.

Friction Block – This looks like a mini deodorant and feels like candle wax. You put it on the areas of your foot where your shoes rub and it allows your strap to slide over without the friction that causes blisters, hence the name Friction Block (though it is often called Blister Block). It definitely works, but I sometimes had to reapply it throughout the day, so I recommend taking it with you in your purse so that you can put it on at any time.

Demi Wispies EyeLashes – These are the most common fake eyelashes used because they can look really full yet natural. They are strips versus individual lashes, which make them easier to apply and remove quickly. You could re-wear them, and in many cases, I have, but they are designed to be disposable.

Brush-On Lash Adhesive – The easiest way to apply your lashes is with a brush-on glue – it's called a "lash adhesive." The brush-on type is similar to a nail polish brush so you aren't dumping glue all over the counter and using a bobby pin to apply it… that was all of us in the 90's. This is sold in clear, white, and dark colors. I prefer the clear or white so I can tell when it's dried, but then you have to go over it with a dark pencil.

Airbrush Leg Makeup – This stuff is amazing! It's like an airbrush foundation for your body! You just gently spray it on your legs and softly spread it over your legs like you would foundation on your face. Don't rub it in because it's not a self-tanner. It's designed to hide your purple veins and even out your skin tone. I wore it to a cocktail party once and my girlfriend complimented me on my pantyhose…I told her pantyhose are for old people, this is airbrush leg makeup. ;)

Wardrobe & Fashion
Sew-in Foam Bra Cups – I fell in love with these sew-in bra cups when I had a cup size smaller than an A. I sewed them into every piece of my competition wardrobe and they not only gave me some gorgeous, proportional oomph, but I didn't have to worry about a bra, bouncing, or switching the same pair between wardrobe. You could even stitch them into your actual bras if you wanted to save yourself $7,000 on plastic surgery – they are that good!

Spanx Power Panties – Spanx are a great product! Not because they hold in fat rolls, which they barely do, but because they even out fat rolls to make your body look even under your clothes. I don't recommend relying on them to give you a great body because there are better ways to actually get a great body. Spanx are on the list because they help evening gowns and interview outfits look smooth even when they are super fitted. It helps soften the thigh jiggle that we all have, plus, it's nice to have something on backstage when you're changing wardrobe. Just be careful because they tend to leave a bodyline at the seams by pressing into the skin. If you wear them too long before your swimsuit walk, it could be ruined by obvious skin dents.

Non-Slip Shoe Sticker – If you don't wear your competition heels outside, which no one really does, then the bottom soles of your shoe will always remain slick. I added these non-slip shoe stickers to the bottom of all of my competition shoes so I didn't have to risk a slip or fall. They even worked great for my jazz shoes for talent when the floor was wooden or tile instead of marley. They are inexpensive and worth it for the peace of mind.

Non-Slip Shoe Insert for Comfort – Use these comfortable gel stickers for the inside of your shoe. They adhere to the inside sole of your shoe and keep the ball of your foot cushioned without sliding forward. There are so many types of these, so find one that works for you and buy a ton of them!

Double-Sided Tape – Double-sided tape is used to tape fabric to fabric, like the lining of your gown or sash to the shoulder of your dress. You won't know that you need it until you put your outfit on and something isn't quite laying right, so have it handy in your backstage kit so you can get to it quickly when the time is right. I haven't found a double-sided tape that worked on my sweaty body to keep a heavily beaded dress from drooping or to keep your bikini from riding, for that, you'll need....

Bikini Butt Glue – It's rather graphic to apply. The best method is to put your bottoms on and visualize where you want them to lay, and then pull them up like you have a wedgie and apply the adhesive. If you're using the roll-on one, make sure you let it dry for 10 seconds or so then, one cheek at a time, gently position your bikini in place. Wherever you put it is where it will stay. I prefer the roll on for precision, but these also come in a spray version. Either way, when you're done with swimsuit competition, use a baby wipe to remove the adhesive before putting on a new outfit or the new outfit will stick to it too!

Practical Products

Hand Steamer – You'll have to have a steamer for your clothing, and my favorite is the e-steam hand steamer. It's so easy to travel with in your suitcase. You fill it with water and plug it in when you arrive. Just be sure to unplug it when you're done so it doesn't catch fire.

Extension Cord/Power Strip –I It seems everyone is fighting for outlets backstage – to charge their phone, to curl their hair, to steam their dress. So most women bring a power strip that they are willing to share with women around them. Make sure you have one for yourself and write your name on it (that's why I like to buy a white one) so that you have priority when you're ready to heat your iron.

Hot-Fix Rhinestone Applicator – For my DIY girl, if you are adding stones to your wardrobe, the best way is with hot-fix stones and this rhinestone applicator. It resembles a glue gun. You plug it in to warm it up and then use the small tip end to lift a rhinestone allowing it to heat the back of the rhinestone where the glue is already placed, then set it into place on your wardrobe and when you lift it up the rhinestone stays glued to the fabric. You can buy these hot-fix rhinestones that come with the ready-to-heat glue on the backs. The alternative is rhinestones that you have to put glue onto, but they are a real pain.

Garment Hanging Rack – sometimes you'll benefit from bringing a garment hanging rack to your pageant. This is especially true if you're sharing a room and you need to share a closet or if your dressing room has limited or no hanging space. Most pageants provide some racks, but it can't hurt to have your own if you can travel with it to your pageant. For small stuff, get the one that is just one bar and bottom shelf, just know they aren't as sturdy as the ones that have a bottom and top shelf.

If you have an extra heavy gown or tons of wardrobe, get the one with the bottom and top shelves.

Not that you have to have all these products to win, but they certainly do relieve a lot of stress during the competition. A full list of these products with links to purchase them on Amazon is available in the free downloadable Beauty, Truth and Grace Guidebook. Get it at: WinAPageant.com/Guide.

61: Packing Protocol for the Pageant Pro

WinAPageant.com/61

Every time we make a decision, we have to use a little piece of energy and willpower. The more decisions we make, the more energy we lose. During your pageant week, you cannot afford to give up unnecessary energy on choosing which earrings to put with which shoes for which outfit. Or bothering with which outfit you meant for Thursday's adventure versus the Friday outing after interview. Too many decisions! This stuff is important, you just need to take care of it before you leave for pageant week.

Pageant girls know that packing for a pageant is no simple task. There are so many things you have to remember. To help you remember everything, I broke down the seven steps of packing like a professional for your pageant, and I'll give a few pro tips to make it even easier.

Step #1 – Map out the number and style of outfits you'll need for the week. How many cocktail dresses, gowns, and rehearsal outfits do you actually need? For example, maybe Monday evening is orientation, so you'll just need an arrival outfit and orientation outfit. Tuesday in the daytime you'll do an appearance at a children's hospital. Then that afternoon you'll have rehearsal and that evening you'll have a cocktail party – that's three outfits right there. After making your list, bring at least one extra cocktail dress, one extra rehearsal/appearance outfit, and one extra competition gown. These are only to be used as backup, not as "options." Remember, the goal of this is to lessen our options.

Step #2 – Once you have the number of outfits you need for each type, I want you to physically lay out the clothing and accessories you'll wear each day. My preference is to not re-wear accessories except for shoes. It helps to re-wear shoes, but not all week, because your feet will be angry. But with jewelry and belts, try to have a new one for each outfit. I'll explain why later.

Step #3 – Now that you have everything laid out, try it all on. Yes, I'm serious. I don't want you to unknowingly forget that you need white underwear for those white shorts or something. Try it all on: bras, jewelry, belts, shoes – everything – and update what you need to so that each outfit is fuss-free. If you have a fussy outfit that you have to always tuck in the hanger tags or keep pulling down the skirt or hike up the neckline – don't wear it. It will distract you and take up too much energy and focus away from your job. I used to cut corners all the time. I would buy a short dress that I'd have to be careful sitting down in, and then the whole day I was just worried about sitting down. When I bought my first pair of heels, I didn't know my size would be smaller than my sneakers, so the pair I bought was way too big. Then I was concerned about walking in them. Trust me, this won't happen to you too many times before you get so sick of it you learn your lesson.

Step #4 – Label your stuff – for others so you don't mix up your Jonathan Kayne shoes with someone else's. And for you, so you remember what you're wearing for what. I would make a notecard for every outfit and describe what I'm wearing for that day (i.e., Navy jump suit, gold necklace, strappy wedges, pink blazer). Then, I'd put a return address label on every zip bag in case I needed to bring the outfit with me for a quick change in between appearances.

Step #5 – Pack in outfits. Put together your zip bag of jewelry, zip of shoes, and zip of clothes. My favorite outfits are ones made of jersey knit material because they don't wrinkle. That's what I take when I travel anywhere for a quick trip, I only take clothes that don't need steamed so I don't have to worry about it. Obviously, you can't have all your outfits be that way for pageantry. But when it comes time to steaming and a few are wrinkle-free, you'll smile at how smart you are and be grateful for an extra seven minutes of sleep.

Step #6 – Hang everything together when you arrive and steam everything so it's done in advance and you aren't rushed for time later. I like to keep my shoes and jewelry in the zipper bag labeled with the day of the week I'm wearing it and the description of the outfit.

Step #7 – When it's been worn, hang it back up so you can re-wear if something else gets messed up. You may have a snafu and have to re-wear the cocktail dress you wore at rehearsal on Monday to the dinner reception on Thursday, or the cocktail dress from Wednesday to sign autographs the day after you win. I'm just saying – stay organized!

Here are a few more tips from the pros:
- Sew foam inserts into any clothing that will need them. Don't try to mess with sticky boobs – they are fussy and don't work that well.
- Have a roller suitcase you can take to rehearsal and the pageant so you don't have to carry a million shoulder bags
- Have one excellent and large shoulder bag for day trips that will fit your crown and sash, shoes, makeup touch-up, and emergency pack.
- Wear wedges or sandals to walk around during sightseeing tours and amusement parks. Of course make sure your shoes are broken in before you go walking five miles around Jacksonville.
- Have slippers and a robe for backstage to get ready in and throw on quickly if you have to run onto stage for an announcement.

The idea behind this packing protocol and the pro tips I shared is to keep you efficient so you are able to make less decisions in the moment and reserve your energy for your pageant win.

16: Managing Pre-Pageant Stress

WinAPageant.com/16

Right before a pageant, it seems chaos comes crashing in. Women get sick and lose their voice, drop their keys in a street drain, break down emotionally, spill coffee on their laps, and get into fender benders. These things aren't normal until it's the month before your pageant. They are a result of extreme stress with your mind whirling around one million things, trying to store details while remaining gorgeous, poised, and striving for perfection every day. I've been there too. I've been so overwhelmed with something larger than me that eventually it boils over into a disaster. I once backed my car into my own garage door before a pageant.

I don't want that to happen to you. So, here are a few basic ways you can manage your stress before it boils over into an all-out disaster.

Tip #1 – Use a to-do list; don't rely on your brain. Your brain is trying to remember so many things; there isn't enough room to remember it all. I keep a note with all the stuff on it and then check it of as I get them done. I also add new things to the list as they come up, but I keep it all in one place – I recommend putting it in the cloud so you aren't also worried about losing a post-it note.

Tip #2 – Do one thing at a time. Time-block what needs to get done and do it. Give yourself exactly enough time to finish a task and 30 minutes rest in between each task. If you need to label your wardrobe, give yourself 60 minutes to do it and a 30-minute break before you start to pack your underwear. Sometimes you'll run over and sometimes you'll just need to turn off your brain and take a few deep breaths. Give yourself plenty of time.

Tip #3 – Have everything prepared at least 10 days before the pageant, because new things will always creep up. Be 100% ready for competition at least one week prior to leaving. That means having your wardrobe back from the tailor, clothes organized, bags tagged, accessories purchased, meal list made, toiletries packed, suitcase set out to go, body in shape. Then, the week before is all about the last minute things and final media push.

Tip #4 – Say "no thanks" to additional responsibilities like planning an event or hosting your nephew's third birthday party. Instead, say, "I'm going to be prioritizing my competition that week, and I think it's better for me to not commit since I don't know what may come up. I want to be sure I don't have to cancel on you at the last minute."

Tip #5 – Prepare for the post-pageant duties. Have all your stuff ready for when you get back, so you don't also have to keep that stuff in your mind. Prepare your thank you cards and press releases. I usually keep a stack of responsibilities for home, school, and work on my desk with a to-do list so when I return (from a pageant or any trip), it's waiting for me with perfect explanation of where I left off with it.

Tip #6 – Relax. Meditate, get a massage, take a bath, do the things that make you take a load off. It'll give you time to reconnect with yourself, your energy, and your Maker so you are confident in your abilities. When I competed, my Aunt Darlene and cousin Mandy always gifted me a massage at our local spa. I loved being able to decompress and release tension before, and sometimes after, the big day.

Bottom line: pay attention to your emotions and how they are effecting your actions. You'll be able to maintain control of your actions if you control your emotions. You can't win a pageant as a ball of stress. When you start feeling like you're having an out-of-body experience, it's gone too far. Jump in a bubble bath with your day planner and start to create an action plan to soothe your stress.

CHAPTER 10

FINISH STRONG

100: Celebrating All Wins

WinAPageant.com/100

My husband, Randy, has a gong in his office that says "Celebrate All Wins" on it. Every time his company has a win they bang the gong. A "win" is any action step they complete that moves them closer to their ultimate goal. The sound of the gong is a declaration of celebration and everyone cheers!

A simple celebration system can be found in many high-achieving companies throughout the world. My chiropractor has a "well bell" that we ring after a great adjustment. When I was a kid, if I had a good check up at the dentist I got to choose a toy from a treasure chest. As an adult, I get a toothbrush just for showing up. In junior high, the class that sold the most zap-it pizzas went on a field trip. Celebrating accomplishments even as an adult is pretty typical. We celebrate graduations, new jobs, promotions, and, of course, pageant wins.

When you celebrate wins, your subconscious seals in a pattern of success. You release dopamine (the feel-good hormone) and your mood and focus increase.

What would happen if you built a pattern of success in the small wins along the way toward your big goal? This is what positive psychologists around the world promote. To accomplish a big goal, you have to successfully complete a series of small tasks and actions as milestones along the way. I call these actions process goals. These are the things you achieve en route toward your big goal – they are a part of your process and they honor the journey toward the destination.

I believe this is the secret sauce of winners. When you celebrate process goals along the path toward your dream, your subconscious becomes trained in a pattern of success. You begin to live life from one celebration to the next.

For example, if you created a series of process goals en route to winning your pageant, they may include things like these: meeting your trainer at the gym three times per week consistently for two consecutive months; securing your first $1,000 of sponsorship funds; completing your wardrobe selection for every phase of competition; launching your platform blog; solidifying a partnership with a relevant charity; and completing a professional mock interview. Do you see how all of these things need to happen along the way to your big pageant win? These are process goals that need to be celebrated to train your brain for success. Achieving each of these doesn't guarantee you a win at your pageant, but without them you're guaranteed to lose.

In 2015, I bought a course that taught me how to launch a podcast. In less than four weeks, I had learned all the steps, set up the technology, wrote and recorded 11 podcasts, designed my artwork, and got approved to produce through iTunes. It was a big project that took a lot of work, but fortunately, I had the full strategy laid out for me in the course and all I had to do was take action. I knew my big goal was to educate and inspire women around the world to win on stage and in life.

When the first episode of the Win A Pageant podcast launched on iTunes that Saturday, Randy took me to his office and cheered as I struck the gong! I'll never forget how good it felt to celebrate that win – the reverberation of the gong in my body, the bright smile Randy had of excitement, and the hope of the future vision coming to pass.

I didn't have any listeners yet, I wasn't even ranked on iTunes, but the first process goal – getting the first batch of podcasts up on iTunes – was complete, and that was worth celebrating!

Flash forward to today, as of the time of writing this, the Win A Pageant podcast has over 40,000 listeners in over 10 countries, ranks as the #1 Pageant Podcast on iTunes and is reviewed at a solid 5-stars. All because I took the course, followed the steps, and launched in the direction of my dreams.

One success leads to another and celebrating your process goals tells your brain that this is a good path and worth your effort.

Right now, wherever you are, you're somewhere between the starting and finishing lines of your big dream. What is the very next step you need to take to move you closer to that dream? Do you need to buy the course? Start the blog? Schedule the interview?

Now is the time to begin. And when you do, be prepared to celebrate all your wins along the way. You don't need a gong. You just need to do something that you'll remember so when you're working toward the next goal, you can smile and know you've made it this far. You could turn on your favorite song and do a wild happy dance, host a movie night with your girlfriends, buy yourself that handbag you've been eyeing, or simply spend an extra 15 minutes in savasana after yoga just to bask in the glory of completeness.

Remember, this is not a race. Just because you're done first, doesn't mean you'll win. That's not how winning works. Winning comes from dedicating yourself to taking action toward your goals and honoring your actions along the way. Don't rush to the finish line. Take time to celebrate all your wins along the way.

12: What Not to Do During Crowning: 7 Don'ts of Your Crowning Moment

WinAPageant.com/12

In an exciting moment like winning a pageant title, you may momentarily lose your wits if you're not wise. When you are standing in the spotlight, whatever impression you leave will last. Perception is reality. You don't want to come off bratty, ungrateful, or just plain crazy. I want to share with you a list of seven things not to do when you're crowned, which will make your winning moment much more graceful, photogenic, and respectable.

Don't #1 – Don't be shocked. Obviously, you'll be excited, and it's great to showcase that emotion (cameras love it!), but you want to be in control of your emotions. I recommend, practicing your crowning moment, so you don't look like a pageant freak that the whole state will be talking about for years. You set out to win, so you shouldn't be shocked when you do.

Don't #2 – Don't miss an opportunity to thank God, your judges, sponsors, family, and friends – remember your roots! When in doubt, over-thank. I love the quote, "A pretty girl can never be too gracious." Everyone that supported you wants to share your success in the lights. If you can get photographs with your family and friends, directors, sponsors, and fellow contestants, do it. They will be proud that they know you and want to share the excitement, so honor them as they've honored you.

Don't #3 – Don't sash yourself; let your predecessor place the sash on you. This is one of the lovely opportunities for the outgoing queen, to be responsible for sashing and crowning you. It's her final responsibility, so please don't steal it from her. Graciously accept her assistance.

Don't #4 – Don't rush. Take your time and soak up the moment. This allows the media to capture lovely photos and you'll have more memories of your crowning moment.

Don't #5 – Don't do a runway walk with a crocked crown. After you've been crowned, stand tall, turn to hug your outgoing queen, look her in the eyes, and ask with a smile, "Is the crown straight?" If not, she'll take a moment to adjust it.

Don't #6 – Don't lock your knees in photos; this is how women pass out. Shift side to side so your knees have a chance to bend and send the blood back to your heart.

Don't #7 – Don't ignore the pageant production team. A whole team of people spent years and thousands of dollars to give you a perfect crowning moment. Be sure to show appreciation to your directors, production team, photographer, stage crew, fellow contestants, choreographer, and so many more for a lovely production.

The beginning of your reign is so important to your continued success. If you accept a title with grace, you'll be seen as graceful.

13: What Not to Do After Winning: 7 Suggestions from My Failures

WinAPageant.com/13

Winning a pageant can be exhilarating, spectacular, overwhelming, exhausting and confusing. People see you as a powerful entity. Superman's dad reminds us that "with great power comes great responsibility." One year goes by very quickly and you have to be prepared to make fast decisions that have the most beneficial impact and do no harm. That's not easy. However, I do have a few specific cautions that I believe will help you to avoid some of the mistakes I've made over the years as a titleholder.

Suggestion #1 – Don't sign anything without reading it. Contracts are written in favor of the author. You should always be given at least 48 hours to review formal contracts and written agreements or consult with an attorney.

Suggestion #2 – Don't shut down your learning sponge. Remain open to learning so you can continue to grow and develop.

Suggestion #3 – Don't stop doing what you did to get what you got. From social media post frequency, how you treat people, learning, listening, and growing. Keep up the great work!

Suggestion #4 – Don't take everyone's advice. It's great to listen to lots of advice, but you must filter through your own truth. If it applies, modify. If not, let it fly.

Suggestion #5 – Don't be used. Draw your line in the sand on your values, your morals, and your desires. You'll have people pulling you in directions you never expected. If you have a moral compass or set of core values to guide you, your decisions will become easier and those around you won't be able to question it.

Suggestion #6 – Don't take anything for granted. If you have a sponsor no matter how large or small, use their products. Look for opportunities to promote them and show your appreciation personally and publically.

Suggestion #7 – Don't forget: the prize is in the process. You won't win every time you compete. If you've only got eyes for the crown, then you will lose out on the experience. The prize is not the crown; the prize is the process.

32: Losing Gracefully

WinAPageant.com/32

In October 2015, I lost my daddy. He had a heart attack and passed away in his sleep. When I got the call, my husband (boyfriend at the time) and I immediately flew home to Pennsylvania to be with my mom. My brother and sisters also flew in and our extended family were all present to hold one another, grieve together, make decisions, and honor my dad's legacy.

The next 10 days were super long. The flood of emotions, lack of sleep, and consistent tears totally wore us all out. When I got back to San Diego, I became painfully aware of the permanence of the loss of my daddy. This is the closest loss I've experienced in my life and this process has taught me so much.

You know that my philosophy of pageantry is that it so closely parallels life. I want to use the lessons I learned from the loss of my dad to share my thoughts on how to lose a pageant with grace. I know these two things seem to be on drastically different levels, but by the end, you'll realize that losing a parent and losing a pageant really are not the end of the world. Plus, you'll have some ways to deal with both more effectively.

Lesson #1 – No one knows what to say. Don't judge their words. Just accept their support.

Lesson #2 – Remember what you've learned. Life is a series of experiences through which you are intended to develop. When you cling to what you've learned from the life experience, you'll realize the good far outweighs the bad.

Lesson #3 – Your support system is vital. Even though they may not know what to say, the people whom you have nurtured will be there to nurture you.

Lesson #4 – Though your world stops, everyone else's keeps turning. Don't blame them and don't blame you.

Lesson #5 – Reflection is powerful. As a pageant coach, I schedule a follow-up call with my VIP clients after their pageant just for the opportunity to reflect. There's much to learn and so much healing that takes place in reflecting after an emotional experience.

Lesson #6 – Give yourself grace. After a loss, it's really awful, all the "what-ifs" that cloud your mind. And at the end of the day, you'll drive yourself crazy with what-ifs. "What if I wore the other gown, what if I did a different talent, what if I'd lived closer, what if I'd called more?" You need to give yourself some grace. You did the best you could with the information you had. Forgive yourself with grace.

Lesson #7 – Everyone handles grief differently. Don't judge other girls based on how they are managing their emotions. You can only be responsible for how you respond. Also, know that likely others are judging you, but that doesn't make it right.

Lesson #8 – Don't fall into the drama pit. It's one thing when your best friend asks how your experience was or your mom asks what you think of the winner, but it's different when a random person tries to get the scoop. There's a difference between curious and nosy. When you lose a pageant, you will have everyone and their brother coming to you for the scoop, trying to create some drama or at the very least be entertained by some. My answer in pageantry is the same, "I guess I wasn't the girl for the job this time." And that's enough to stay drama-free and keep your emotions away from the dark "what-ifs."

Lesson #9 – Emotions aren't an indicator of truth. Emotion is energy in motion, meaning it will eventually move on. That's why you shouldn't make decisions on little sleep or a hungry stomach. The same is true after a loss. After the loss of my dad, we were all thinking wacky.

One of my dad's friends who had experienced loss in the past advised my mom to make no major decisions for at least two years. In pageantry, two years may be excessive, but at least two weeks would be wise. Confused minds shouldn't make important decisions. When emotions are high, intelligence is low.

Lesson #10 – It's okay to get back on the horse. One day you'll have to come to terms with the reality of losing and decide to get back on the horse, back into the game, back to your routine and back to your life.

Lesson #11 – Romans 8:28 promises, "All things work together for good for those who love God and are called according to His purpose." Even in this difficult time, I have to know that God is going to set this exact situation up for something spectacular for me (because I love Him) and for everyone in our family because we all love God. God's promises aren't empty. My hope is in my future – I can't wait to see how God works this together for good.

15: The Anatomy of a Proper Thank You

WinAPageant.com/15

Showing gratitude is proper etiquette for those with good social graces. But just saying "thanks" or sending a text really isn't sufficient for your gratitude to be truly felt. And we know that the more grateful you are in your response to generosity, the more generous people are.

I always go above and beyond for my clients. Mostly because it's what I love – I get all jazzed up when I see them succeeding! But for the clients that regularly show gratitude, I am always looking for ways to over-deliver with generosity. Giving feels good when it's well received. If you can show you appreciate someone's generosity, they're far more likely to continue giving.

Thank you notes aren't trained on in school. Most people never learn to write a good note, yet are delighted when they receive one.

My mom is the one who taught me to write thank you notes. It's an amazing skill. Our notes were timely, personal, significant, and thoughtful. Truthfully, at the time, writing a thank you note was a real pain. Each Christmas we had to write about 15 notes to family members who lived next door even though we saw every day anyway. My mom always said that they wouldn't know I appreciated their gift unless I told them.

It was hard to comprehend this concept, mostly because at age 8 I had never given a thoughtful gift and received a beautiful note of gratitude. Nor had I given a thoughtful gift and heard nothing, which is also a powerful lesson in gratitude. It wasn't until I started giving thoughtful gifts and being generous that I started receiving thank you cards. And let me tell you – I get the biggest smile on my face each time I receive a card! That's why I find it so valuable to show gratitude to those that are appreciated.

I have one client in particular, Erin, who writes me the most beautiful thank you cards! She lives nearby my hometown and must have had a mother like I do because her cards are always timely, personal, significant, and thoughtful. I received one recently and got her permission to share it on my site, so if you would like to see an example of an amazing thank you note, go to WinAPageant.com/15 to read Erin's.

I'm going to walk you through the anatomy of a thank you card so that you can write amazing words to those you are grateful for and show them how much you appreciate their generosity.

First, be sure your note is:

- Timely – within one week, though late is better than never
- Personal – speak directly to the gift that was given and how you'll use it
- Significant – more than one or two sentences
- Thoughtful – think beyond the words "thank you"

Secondly, there are four things to include in your notes:

1. How did this gift make you feel?
2. Why is this gift so valuable? Or what will you do with it?
3. Statement of Thanks
4. Compliment to honor the giver

A simple example may be: "I felt so loved to see you attending the pageant. The flowers you brought were lovely and are still blooming beautifully on my dining room table. Thank you for your thoughtfulness and generosity! I'm lucky to have a friend like you in my life to support my hobbies with so much love!"

My clients like Erin, Samantha, Kristina, Rachel, Lori and Emaleigh send me thoughtful notes, messages, and social media posts that make me want to do more for them! I find myself shipping off cocktail dresses, earrings, clothing, little presents and cards to my clients regularly – at least the ones that I can tell appreciate it. Generosity that brings gratitude brings more generosity.

50: Pageant Resale: How to Sell Your Used Pageant Wardrobe

WinAPageant.com/50

The best time to capitalize on pageant resale – whether you're buying or selling – is spring and summer when pageant season is in full swing. I'm going to share with you tips to consider when you prepare to re-sell your used pageant wardrobe so you can sell it fast and for a fair price without having to give it away (although, I have an opinion about this that I'll share with you later). We'll cover knowing your customer, how to showcase it best, how to price your item, and how to ship it with grace.

Tip #1 – Know Your Customer

Let's start with the end in mind: your customer. This is the person who will ultimately end up buying your used wardrobe. Most of the women that are buying resale items are competing in local or state pageants. It's rare that you'll get a future Miss USA or Mrs. International buying a used gown, though that has happened. Buyers are rarely in their in-it-to-win-it year, but they are very concerned about exact color, fit, and shipping costs. It is vital to be absolutely clear in your posting so that you have happy customers. It's also important to speak their language. You're not going to sell a gown to a pageant woman that says, "It didn't score well, so I'm selling it." Trust me. No one will buy it. Instead, be honest, but leave your personal opinion of the gown out of the equation.

Tip #2 – Showcase Right

Most sites will require you to upload pictures of your wardrobe and a description. I recommend using photos you take yourself rather than the ones from the designer's website. Of course, you want them to be great pictures, but you don't want them to seem too good to be true or people won't trust you. If you have images of the dress on stage – even better! Plus, it helps to see a real human in the dress so the buyer can estimate size. In the description, include details of size, color, and any blemishes – even small ones. If some of the beading is undone on the backside, mention it and upload a specific picture showing that.

Tip #3 – Price Right

Pricing should start at 50% of the purchase price. This is because the dress is likely at least a season old, plus it has been worn and maybe even altered. If nothing else is different (no stains, no missing beads, no odd custom dimensions), then 50% is perfect. If there are other issues with the dress, consider taking off additional dollar amounts based on what the customer will need to do to fix the gown.

A Side Note about Super-Low Pricing:

Let me suggest to you that if you own a gown that you bought for $100 or less, instead of trying to resell the gown for $50, just give it to someone close to you that could benefit from it. I've given out countless cocktail dresses and prom gowns to pageant girls just getting started in their pageant career – these have gone a long way! My clients can attest to getting a text from me saying, "Would you wear this if I sent it to you?" I love seeing their pictures on social media in my wardrobe with a little wink-y face saying, "Thanks Alycia!" It makes me feel good to sow into their pageant career. As you know, pageant women always need gowns for appearances, and it is such a treasure when someone you know gives you a dress. So don't be the girl that nickels and dimes people. When you are blessed, be a blessing to someone else.

Tip #4 – Ship Right

Once you have a buyer (or someone to give the dress to), ensure the dress is freshly cleaned and ship it immediately. Some buyers wait until the last minute to purchase the gown and then track it every half hour until it arrives, so they'll appreciate your haste. Finally, package your product like you are sending a fine wine to the Queen of England. I wrap gowns in tissue paper and put them in a priority box with the buyer's name clearly handwritten with love and enclose a sweet note letting them know the dress was good to me and that I know it will be good to them too. A great buying experience goes a long way.

51: Pageant Resale: Where to Resell Your Pageant Wardrobe

WinAPageant.com/51

Here are some important factors to consider when choosing a site from which to sell your pageant wardrobe:

1. Fee to list and sell
2. Size of audience
3. Insurance/Guarantee
4. Ease of use
5. Readiness to ship

In general, sites that provide an opportunity for reselling make money from the seller because they are providing you the forum to sell and the marketing. It's either on the front end by charging a flat listing rate or on the back end by charging either a flat rate or, more commonly, a percentage of the money you make. If you're selling a $100 cocktail dress, 6% is $6. If you're selling a $1,000 gown, it's $60. If the flat rate is $6 per month and you're selling a $1,000 gown, that could be a better deal for you as the seller. So do your math.

If you have a low risk tolerance or you don't know if it will sell, the safe route is to only pay when you get paid. However, this doesn't mean that these sites bring the highest traffic volume of potential buyers to view your wardrobe.

For that, consider the size of the audience. If there are a lot of people on a particular Facebook group, a lot of activities, and you see "Sold" next to many of the dresses, these could be good signs that the site has been successful.

Another important aspect is a seller and/or buyer guarantee or insurance – eBay has this feature. If there's a problem with the product not being delivered on time or as per the post, or if the buyer's payment bounces, there are steps in place to protect both parties. It's a lot better than shipping someone a piece and then waiting an eternity for them to never send you a check. Or to buy a dress when the buyer tells you they'll have it to you in a week and it never arrives. See what I mean? This is important.

The ease of the transaction is vital. The backend of any web transaction is extremely complex, but they are designed to be secure and smooth. If it's not, don't use it. For me, eBay is very confusing. I've sent two used cell phones out to buyers on eBay before they confirmed the purchase and one changed his mind about wanting it at all. That wasn't eBay's fault. I jumped in too soon and didn't know what I was doing. So be sure you are comfortable with the site, the process, and the payments before committing to anything.

Finally, your timing is crucial. Don't post something on a site if you aren't able to ship it when someone buys it. If you're going out of town for two weeks or you have the flu or it's tech week for your dance school, it may be tough to watch your email for questions and purchases. Be ready for someone to buy it – cleaned, packaged, and prepared to ship immediately.

On the website (WinAPageant.com/51), there is a list of 10 websites and several Facebook groups for you to consider when buying or selling used wardrobe. There are consignment shops, eBay types, and even wardrobe rental options. I haven't used any of these myself so I can't speak from personal experience, but I know that it has worked for many pageant sisters. But please do your due diligence to vet these to make sure it's right for you. It's definitely a fun experience to see someone in the same gorgeous gown you only wore once. It makes you want to cheer for them extra loud!

CHAPTER 11

BE THE BEST TITLEHOLDER

92: How to Become a Pageant Star

WinAPageant.com/92

One thing that is obvious to most pageant women is that in order to win your pageant, you have to truly be a star. When you meet a star, you'll know it, but it's hard to explain what it really means to be a star. It's also evident when it's not there, when something is missing – even if you can't quite put your finger on what exactly is missing.

Every single woman in the Miss Universe pageant from 86 countries around the world is a celebrity. They are stunningly beautiful models. They have bright smiles, graceful walks, and incredible hair. But, not all of them are stars.

In an interview after the pageant, one judge was asked why a certain contestant (who seemingly had the whole package) didn't make it into the finals. The judge simply said that something was missing. The host asked what was missing. The judge said, "Well I don't know, but something just wasn't there."

That something, I believe, is the star quality. Just as tough as it is to explain the star quality, it's even harder to know whether or not you have it. Although it's noticeable to everyone else, it may not be to you.

Do you truly have the star quality necessary to win your pageant and take your message to the top? I have great news: everyone has the potential to exude this star quality – you do, too.

I'm going to unpack exactly what this star quality looks like through the analogy of a real star in the galaxy. Then, I'm going to explain how being a star brings you to the top. Finally, I'm going to break down how you can exude that star quality to get to the top.

First, let me compare for you a star in outer space with a woman who is a true pageant star to show the similarities. For the sake of this analogy, let's use a star from far off in our galaxy.

Similarity #1 – A star in the galaxy is a bright beam of natural burning gas that radiates light that can be seen from a far distance. A pageant star is someone who radiates light from a far distance. It can be seen from miles away. She simply walks into a room and brightens it up. People notice her.

Similarity #2 – A star in the galaxy is always there, shining brightly no matter who is looking (because someone is always looking). The best time to see it is when your side of the world is covered in darkness, when the sun is gone. When the sun comes up for you, the other part of the world is in darkness and that star is shining there for those people. In the pageant world, presence is vital. A pageant star is a woman who is ready to say, "yes" to travel wherever she is needed most. From early morning hours to late nights, the pageant star has to be ready to serve the world around her.

Similarity #3 – A star in the galaxy burns from natural energy and doesn't turn off until it dies. Pageant stars are the same! These women have a natural fuel keeping them passionate, serving, and forward moving all the time. A true pageant star needs this natural fuel otherwise she'd be exhausted trying to fake it. A true pageant star is a woman who's light shines brightly, not from her own power, but a natural source within her, and is able to be seen even in the darkest situation.

So to recap, a star has three defining features: it can be seen from a far distance, it is always there, and it is fueled by a natural energy.

Consider a lamp. No one turns on a lamp and then puts it under a basket. They light the lamp and put it on a table so it will light the whole house. The Bible points this out in Matthew 5:15, right after it says that YOU are the light of the world.

You. Sitting where you are right now. You, my dear, are the light of the world. God wants you to shine! Why? Because He knows that if you are shining, people will put you up on a table, girl! No one will hide you in a basket. THIS is why people elevate star quality. They can't help but put the lamp on the table to light the whole house.

I promise you this: if you let your light shine, you will be placed on top. You are designed to be the head and not the tail. Above and not beneath. God said, "You are the light of the world." Let it shine, sister!

"How?" You ask. Simple: shine light. Light is basically everything that is positive. "Whatever is true, noble, whatever is right, pure, lovely, admirable – if anything is excellent or praiseworthy – think about such things." (Philippians 4:8)

Do not let negative, fear-based, anxious, nasty, condescending, or untrue lies leave your lips. That is darkness. You are called to be the light.

Do the right thing. Help people in need. Say nice things that lift people up and light up their spirits. Be lovely and be pure. Think about excellent things. Think, act, and speak things that are worthy of praise.

Imagine that every time you do something that is noble, right, pure, lovely, admirable or excellent, a handful of sparkling glitter falls from the sky and sticks to you, following you around everywhere you go. The more glitter you throw around the brighter your light shines.

Now, just because it's simple doesn't mean it's easy. It's not. You have an adversary working against you. Always coming at you with evil, unkind, nasty thoughts about you, your circumstances, and others around you. These nasty thoughts make you want to act nasty and then create more nastiness around you.

You have to throw glitter around from a source that is not your own. This is where you're going to need God's grace. When those nasty thoughts come into your mind, you need to refuel with God. The best way to do this is to repeat the mantra, "I am the light of the world. I am the light of the world." This is in Matthew 5:14 if you want to look it up. When you anchor back to this mantra, it acts as a sword to cut out the evil thoughts and replace it with noble, pure, positive thoughts.

Although it is a simple concept, it is not so easy to implement which is why not everyone is a star. Still, you are called to do this, and I sincerely hope you will accept this challenge. I want you to be a pageant star! I want you to be the woman that lights up a room, that everyone is drawn to, and when a judge asks why you, she says, "I don't know, she just had this certain quality about her." I want glitter to stick to your whole entire body and shine light around the entire world!

I know God wants this for you too. You have a call on your life to be great and you need to be put up on the table. Let your light shine so the whole world will see. Remember that song from when you were a kid, "This Little Light of Mine"? This is a great one to get stuck in your head every morning. I have a wonderful rendition of this song on the site at WinAPageant.com/92 that will bring you to beautiful, empowered tears.

Shine your light, my dear. Shine it brightly, all the time, no matter where you are or whom you are with, fueled on God's promise: "You are the light of the world."

69: 7 Steps to Book a Pageant Appearance

One common misconceptions of winning a pageant is the idea that when you win, you'll be swept away into some fairytale land where you get a business manager, public relations specialist and full glam team. The reason people believe this is because this is what happens in some of the big-name pageants. But, for most pageant winners, this is not the case, in fact when you win your pageant you are actually expected to be the one to book your own appearances. Sometimes you are contractually obligated to do 2 or more per month, so this is a necessary skill to learn long before you win the title.

Of course, before you can even begin to book appearances you have to know your brand and have a solid understanding of your platform and Legacy Project so you know where your skills will best align. I'm going to share with you the seven steps to book appearances like a true pageant professional – with or without a crown.

Step #1 – Research Related Partners

The first step of the process is to research related partners such as, organizations, groups or businesses that align with the same mission that you are supporting. I suggest starting with the yellow pages and a good ole Google search. You might even find local chapters of national organizations like the Rotary Club, the Girl Scouts, schools or libraries in your area that could support or benefit from your platform and Legacy Project. Make a list of the possible partners that you find in a Google or Excel spreadsheet. Include the name of the organization the name of the person that you would contact, their actual contact information, and any notes that you take when you actually do reach out to them. This will help you keep everything organized so you can track the progress that you're making.

Step #2 – Offer Something Valuable

When you actually do reach out to these contacts that you've researched you have to offer them something of value. Consider what is important to them. Is there a certain initiative that they are promoting in this moment? Or maybe there is a common market that they are trying to reach to which you have direct access.

For example, when I was working closely with the American Heart Association I was in contact with several public schools because I was a certified teacher with an approved background check, which every volunteer needed. My mom and dad also worked in the public school system, so we had contacts in many districts. That was valuable to the American Heart Association and therefore allowed me to work with them for many appearances in elementary schools and college campuses.

Think about what you can bring to the table. Sometimes non-profit organizations seek volunteers that are available to host tables at health fairs, be present to give out sandwiches at fundraising walks, and give talks within a specific region on a topic of interest. Maybe you have a flexible schedule or experience in a certain sport. These are your strengths.

When you contact an organization share your strengths in a way that they can benefit from. You may say something like, "Hi my name is Alycia and I'm interested in volunteering for your organization. I'm a public speaker and a certified teacher and I love to work with children. Who would be the best person for me to talk to about volunteer positions with your organization?"

Notice how I started with what's important to them rather than saying, "Hi my name is Alycia, I am Miss so-and-so and I want to get into the schools to talk to the children." Anytime you need somebody to be on your side, approach the conversation from their side of the table.

Step #3 – Get Contact Info and Follow Up

The next thing that you want to do is leave your contact information. Many organizations have an ongoing list of possible volunteers that they reach out to for various activities when needed. You want to be on that list!

It may also be wise for you to talk directly to whoever is the volunteer coordinator or whoever is responsible for booking the type of volunteering that you want to provide.

For example if you want to give a speech at a Rotary Club meeting, you need to be aware of who books those speakers. You'll get their specific contact information and that's who you'll follow up with until they tell you no, or you are invited to an appearance. When you're invited – respond immediately – that's step #4!

Step #4 – Respond Immediately

My recommendation is to respond to somebody's outreach or invitation within 24 hours. I used to be on a call list to speak to groups in Los Angeles on behalf of the American Heart Association. Los Angeles, as you can imagine has no shortage of speakers, so when I got an email request, I had to jump on it within a matter of hours to secure the position. It's important that you are on top of your communication; whether it is to ride in the parade, speak on behalf of an organization, attend a fundraiser, or write a guest blog, that level of professionalism goes a long way. In your response call, gather some information to understand their needs and the specific details.

Step #5 – Confirm Details 3-7 Days Before

Now that you know exactly what to expect and you have prepared for the event you should confirm the details at least 3 days before the event and up to a full week before depending on the size of the event. Send a very brief email with the basics of the details that you have and what you are expecting to deliver in terms of time, attire and presentation on the given day. For example, if you are selling roses at a black tie gala your details will include the fact that you will be wearing a formal gown arriving at 4:30 p.m. and bringing a white basket for the roses. I have found that it's better to include this level of detail. This gives them the grace of knowing they may have missed telling you something and they can fill in those blanks. Even if your details are as simple as arriving at 147 Oak Avenue at 11 a.m. with a Corvette, magnetic signs and printed formal introduction of you for the MC of the parade - still confirm the details as you understand them.

Step #6 – Be Spectacular

My client Brianne who recently won her state pageant, came to my house for her VIP day and we developed this concept of being paid $20,000 to walk around on stage for 3 minutes each time. She created that vision for each phase of competition, showing up with her best self, putting aside any negative self-talk and owning the stage for those 3 minutes. She obviously nailed it and won! The same strategy will work for your appearance. If you imagine yourself being paid $20,000 to just show up for whatever appearance you're doing, I bet you'd be spectacular! That's what you want to deliver – your very best self. Get plenty of rest, put yourself together so you look fantastic, show up early, bring an extra dress, your talent cd, or a spare microphone just in case. Be ready to save the show, step into whatever role they give you and be worth $20,000. Everyone you interact with will be asking, "how did they book her?" and "I wonder how much it will cost to get her at my event?" I promise your excellence will pay off.

Step #7 – Follow Up

Within 48 hours after the event follow up with a thank you note. I'm sure you know by now that gratitude is high on my values list. I love sharing my appreciation with the people around me and I have found that the more appreciation I show the more generosity others give. When you follow up with a handwritten thank you note you will find that opportunities are continually brought to you. Send a thank you note to your Corvette driver, one to the newscaster who interviewed you on camera, definitely one to the contact that help you set everything up. Even the volunteer coordinator at the day of the event would appreciate your gratitude. I sometimes even send photographs of myself and the volunteer coordinator or other key players so that they remember who I am and of course have a keepsake of the event. This is how you ensure that the reputation for your work is glowing and grow your network.

The longer your list of contacts the more opportunities you will be able to create for yourself (even before your pageant) and more powerful the impact you'll make at your pageant.

53: 7 Must-Know Pageant Etiquette Tips to Protect Your Reputation

WinAPageant.com/53

Most women learn pageant etiquette as they go through the process of pageantry, generally because someone else does something that they really respect or they do something that everyone else disrespects and points it out. This has happened to me, and I'm sure it's happened to you because it happens to all of us. Do not fret. I'm about to teach you a few things that will save you a lot of embarrassment.

Etiquette Tip #1 – Your Full Title

It's easy to know how to introduce yourself when you're Miss USA. You just say, "I'm Miss USA." But what about if you are Miss Greater Lakes of the North International Teenager of America US. It's a little more complex, wouldn't you say? You're going to want to say Miss Greater Lakes or Miss GL of the North so you don't run out of breath with your complex title. But different pageants have different titles to signify which pageant system the titleholder belongs to. If you shorten your title, it could be confusing to the audience (or infringe on trademark laws). The rule is, when you formally introduce yourself, use your full title as it was announced when you received the crown, even if it's super-long.

Etiquette Tip #2 – "Thank You"

The second most common etiquette error happens just after responding to an on-stage question. Contrary to what often happens, you should not finish your statement with "Thank you." A presidential candidate doesn't finish every answer at a press conference with "Thank you." Therefore, neither should you. The exception to this is if the audience is going truly wild with applause for some marvelous thing you just said. I've seen it a time or two before where a woman answers a question in such a witty and amazing way that the audience truly goes wild with applause, and in this case, it is totally appropriate to thank them for applauding your opinion. Otherwise, simply bringing your gaze back to the person that asked the question and sewing up your answer with a finishing tone of voice is proper etiquette.

Etiquette Tip #3 – Gown Shopping

Our next piece of etiquette comes from gown storeowners around the globe. Every time you enter a pageant gown store, you should act like you just walked into Dolce and Gabbana on Rodeo Drive. By that I mean, calm down, go slow, and treat everything with care. When you flip through the racks, handle the gown by the hangers not the fabric, which could damage the gown or leave marks from oils on your hands. Take only three to five gowns into the dressing room at a time and hang each one up before you take another off the hanger. Don't try things on over your tank top or ask to try a new pair of earrings with each gown. Instead, be thoughtful in the process and respect the gowns and the attendants helping you. They are there to make sure the gowns are lovely. Treat them with respect and they will respect you.

Etiquette Tip #4 – Store Discounts

Sometimes you'll receive a discount or a gift card to spend at a merchant's store. This is common as a part of a pageant prize package. The store discount is intended to put toward a larger purchase, not for a free cocktail. If you receive $200 to a store as a gift, please do not show up to the store expecting to redeem it without at least buying a pair of shoes. For a business owner, this level of sponsorship is a marketing strategy. Most gown stores that give discounts are deeply tied to the pageant, and the owners and attendants are excited to have you in their store so they can show you the unique merchandise they have. If you show up searching for something no more than $195, they won't view you in a positive light. Instead, when you are ready to buy additional wardrobe (and there is always a time for another cocktail dress, gown, shoes, and accessories), that's a perfect time to shop with them. If you do end up finding the perfect dress for $199, at least buy a pair of shoes and earrings to make it worth their time and generosity.

Etiquette Tip #5 – Gift Giving

Gift giving is a huge part of pageantry. It is totally appropriate to bring a generous gift for your pageant roommate, host family, parents, sponsors, and directors; plus a little something small for each of the other contestants and back-stage volunteers. I know many women give gifts like they are passing out beads at Mardi Gras, but I always prefer to give gifts privately so that the true meaning of the gesture isn't confused with showing off.

Etiquette Tip #6 – Talking to Judges

Immediately after a pageant, there are tons of emotions flying around, even for the judges. Many times they didn't want that girl to win either, they were rooting for you the whole time. Or they think you had no shot, but have a million ideas of what they wish they could have said to you. Either way, this is not the time nor place to get into that conversation. A simple and genuine "thank you for taking the time to be here today to judge the pageant" will go a long, long way! You can always follow up with them later.

Etiquette Tip #7 – Always Thank Your Sponsors

Everyone who has sewn into your experience deserves a thank you note – the directors, production staff, host hotel, judges, sponsors, and authors of books you've read (eh, hem ;)) – even the people you've paid, like your gown designer, stylist, coach, and paperwork editor. I recommend keeping a list as you prepare so you can show your gratitude after the big event with a gift or at least a hand-written thank you note.

There are a lot of etiquette tips you'll learn throughout your pageant journey. Most importantly, seek advice from people you trust, ask for feedback, and always remain humble.

77: 4 Steps to a Celeb-Style Pageant Bio

WinAPageant.com/77

I want to make you sound like a true celebrity. Not that you're not, it's just that sometimes when you write a boring bio and someone reads it from stage, you sound boring. I'm going to teach you how to write an epic pageant bio that makes you sound like the celeb you are!

Step #1 – Write a list of all the things that make you awesome. Think of awards, titles, positions you've held. This could be that you are a brand ambassador for an organization or the secretary of the National Honor's Society. Or you could talk about how you wrote a book, created an app, designed a t-shirt, raised money, or founded a student club. Write out your tidbits of awesomeness in bullet points (not full sentences yet).

Step #2 – Put the bullet points in order of how awesome they sound to others. If someone read them out in one of those announcer voices, which one is the coolest? Practice in your best radio voice: "Born in New Orleans," "sophomore at Florida State University," "Weekly Relationship Columnist at the local tribune," "Creator of the women's fashion blog Rocking Robes." Get what I mean? When you say it in an announcer voice, the silly things sound silly and the cool stuff sounds really cool! That's what will help you determine the difference. So put them in order of greatness with the top one being the most compelling.

Step #3 – Write one sentence for every bullet point with the focus on the actual accomplishment. For example, if you created a blog don't write your sentence like this: "She created a blog called Rocking Fashion." Instead say this: "She's the creator of the online fashion resource for women called Rocking Fashion." See what I did there? Make it fancy!

Step #4 – Go back through each of your sentences and give each one a different starting phrase to make them sounds unique and avoid redundancy. You don't want every sentence to start with "She is the…" Instead, try rewriting the sentence starting with "Her…" and "As the…" to describe your accomplishments.

I want to share with you an actual bio of one of my clients, Rita. Rita is a rock star and she wrote her own bio the first time. Then, I wrote her bio and showcased her actual rock star-isms and it made a world of difference for her press kit!

Her original was:
"Born in Japan, to a military father and native Japanese mother, Rita was always told that she should use her strengths to help others. As someone who was very interested in technology and entrepreneurship early on in life, she loved empowering others by helping people learn about technology and entrepreneurship. She was scammed in high school when trying to create an app, and wants to use her knowledge and skillset to help others with their goals."

I rewrote it to read:
"Rita Roloff is a national Ambassador for Pretty Brainy and founder of StilletosToStem.com, where she inspires women to learn technology. She's a tech expert who's seen and tried it all from app development to fashion-tech design. You can find her online doing regular Facebook Live videos about the latest in tech. Rita is currently studying tech entrepreneurship at UW-Madison."

A few key takeaways from this example are that we focused on the most important aspects and left out the boring details. We also only used words with positive connotation. Help your audience, judges, and fans see your best aspects and leave them with a positive, uplifted feeling.

49: Make Your Autograph Cards Impressive and Functional

WinAPageant.com/49

Every pageant titleholder has to have autograph cards, not just as a give-away at children's events. The autograph cards are vital marketing pieces for your year and must be created as such. You'll use your autograph cards similarly to business cards, thank you cards, and flyers, so there are certain things that should always be included.

What to Include on Your Autograph Cards

1. Headshot: The photo should look like you. Since you'll be giving these out in person, you want people to remember you and know how to get in touch. Also, make sure it's on a white background so you can write a message and sign it – don't use a photo with a black or dark background or wild colors all over. Trust me, it's limiting.

2. Name: Of course, your name needs to be included (you'd be surprised how many women forget this).

3. Title: Your title isn't necessary, unless your pageant is buying the cards in which case they will want it on there. If you are going on to a national pageant, you don't want to have 2,000 cards that say "Miss Macomb" if in 3 months you could become Miss Illinois and eventually Miss America, right? With that said, all state, national, and international titleholders will use their title on their cards.

4. Year: The year is also optional. It's great if you won't reuse them, but I was often told to bring 200 autograph cards and ended up using three. So listing the year is potentially wasteful. Be smart, but don't over-do it.

5. Website: A place where people can learn more about you and your cause.

6. Social Media Tags and Hashtags: Where and how people can connect with you.

7. Platform concept, title, logo, website, points of interest.
8. Personal brand slogan: This is for the advanced pageant titleholders. It's the best way for people to connect you to future opportunities.

Now, let's talk about how to design this. You could hire a professional designer to manage the layout, or just use a design resource to create it yourself! I use Canva.com to create custom designs. I like to create a rough draft of my ideas here to send to a pro so they can see my vision.

You have to also know the size of the print you want because that will impact the design. I prefer 5x7 postcard prints because they are less likely to be lost and easy to print at just about any printing source. I use Vistaprint.com because they are affordable, high quality, and offer fast shipping.

How to Design Your Cards

Front: On the front is your headshot and name (and year and title if you are including this information)

Back: On the back is where you put the info you want to share with people and specific action you want them to take. You could also put your social media, website, slogan, and anything else here.

Bring these with you everywhere you go and don't be shy using them to promote your platform and yourself for additional appearances. Give them to children and adults. Be proud of them! Autograph cards say a lot about a titleholder. You want it to communicate that you are professional, personable, and engaging. Then, when it gets into the hands of the right person like a potential sponsor, platform partner, media pro, or some other action-taker: BAM! Suddenly that 25-cent piece that you put a lot of thought into becomes a huge opportunity provider!

You can look at an example of my autograph cards online at: WinAPageant.com/49.

38: Grace, The Greatest Gift of All

WinAPageant.com/38

"Graceful" is the word frequently used to describe pageant women as they glide across the stage or move like a ballet dancer. But "grace" has a much more powerful meaning.

Socially, when someone "gives someone grace," they are essentially looking past their flaws. If a public speaker got up to deliver a keynote speech and she had a cold that distorted her voice, she may say, "I'm a little sick today, so I appreciate your grace." Meaning, "don't judge me."

Grace is giving someone something wonderful that they do not deserve. This is not to be confused with mercy, which is to remove something evil from someone who does deserve the consequence of it. These terms are frequently mixed up because they originated in the Bible when talking about what Jesus did for human kind.

Jesus provided both deliverance from evil and the gift of salvation. In the original text of the Bible, the word "grace" was used to reference these and through translation, the gift of saving someone from evil has turned into not giving someone evil, which is mercy.

Right now, we're talking about actual grace – where it came from, how to get it, and how to give it. If you can cultivate grace and learn to express it on stage and in your interview, you'll be seen as exhibiting love, truth, and hope. And if you are the only contestant oozing love, truth, and hope – who can stop you?

Where Grace Came From

In the Old Testament (which is the events that happened before Jesus), God was seen as judgmental. If you did something wrong, you were condemned. If you've ever seen The Bible Series (on YouTube or Netflix), you can relate to the terror of the day. It's so barbarian, but makes sense.

You may remember the story of Moses who first leads his people out of Egypt after many plagues, and then goes up to the top of a mountain and receives The 10 Commandments struck on stone by

God. That was considered "the law" so people obeyed these rules and if you didn't, you were sinning. "For the law was given through Moses; grace and truth came through Jesus Christ." (John 1:17)

Of course, people were always sinning because no one was perfect, so as a symbol of repentance from your sins back then, every week you were to bring a "perfect" lamb to the temple as a sacrifice. You'd pass over your lamb or goat or whatever you had and the priest would inspect the lamb to make sure it didn't have any blemishes, like dark spots or scars or other weird things that animals could have. As long as the lamb was spotless, they would accept it. They killed it and you were redeemed and forgiven from your sins.

Notice, they never asked what your sins were. Only you and God knew that. The priest didn't care. They didn't inspect you; they only inspected the lamb.

Many years later, a young girl named Mary was engaged to a man named Joseph. The bible says Mary was a virgin, yet she became pregnant, because God is amazing. The town then rejected her because she was not yet married, but she was pregnant. So Mary and Joseph left the town, and on their journey, Mary started having contractions and was about to have the baby. They stopped at an Inn in Bethlehem, but it was full (I imagine inns then were probably more like bed and breakfasts than the Hilton), so the innkeeper offered them shelter in his barn. That's where Mary gave birth to Jesus! (You can read all the details of this in Matthew, Chapter 1.)

God wanted Mary to have Jesus because he was going to spread a new message – one of love, truth, hope, and grace. During Jesus's young life on Earth – he only lived on this planet into his 30's – people still would slaughter lambs to have their sins forgiven. When he was an adult, Jesus was talking about being the Son of God. The powerful people of the time were worried that if His following grew, they'd take over the government, so they arrested him for "blasphemy" (apparently that was a crime back then). Then they put him through hideous pain and ridicule. I think this was because they wanted to make an example of him, so people didn't keep spreading Jesus's message (but our God is bigger than people's intimidation so it didn't work anyway).

I'm summarizing and simplifying thousands of years of history to make my point. It's coming, hang in there. Jesus was crucified, which means killed, hanging from a cross next to two actual criminals. The Bible says there was one moment when he screamed, "Father, why have you forsaken me?" Which means, "Dad, why did you leave me?" This was the one moment that all the sin of the world came onto Jesus. Because God cannot be where there is sin, they were separated. Jesus died as the ultimate perfect lamb so that people no longer had to slaughter lambs for forgiveness. His soul had no blemishes, so He could take on the sins of the world. He did that by dying for you and me.

Because of this hideous and yet beautifully loving moment, you and I get to come every day to God with our perfect lamb, Jesus. God inspects the lamb and then accepts him so we don't have to suffer. You are given both mercy (you don't have to be crucified) and grace (you get to go to Heaven)! Jesus is the ultimate present you get to unwrap every day – His grace covers every blemish you have.

How to Get Grace

You have to actually unwrap the present. Someone can hand you a gorgeous turquois box wrapped with white ribbon, but if you don't open it, you'll never wear the Tiffany's bracelet. Even if you do open it, you could shove the bracelet in a drawer and it'll do you no good unless you wear it.

The same is true of Jesus's grace. You have to unwrap it by asking him to give it to you, use it once to get you started, and then use it every day. The guilt and shame that comes with sins I've committed is instantly washed away when I talk to God about removing my sins. He actually makes me feel brand new again.

The way you do it is through conversation with God called prayer. It's basically talking to God like you would a friend. How you talk to

God is totally unique to you and Him. If you haven't done it before, here's a good one to start with:

Dear Lord, I want to thank You that You love me so much, You sent Jesus Christ, Your only son, to die on the cross to wash away all my sin and set me free. Today, I am forgiven because of Your sacrifice. Today, Lord Jesus, I turn my heart to You. Come into my life and fill me with Your Spirit. Make me Your child from this day forward. I declare: You are Lord over my life, Heaven is my home, and God is my father in Jesus mighty name. Amen.

How to Give Grace

You give grace the same way you give any present. If you have a special present and you never tell anyone about it, like you don't put a tag with their name on it, you don't hand it to them, or you never mention you have a gift for them, they don't know about it. You have to talk about it! Giving someone grace feels like a warm hug. It's non-judgmental, non-confrontational; it's just an opportunity for someone to feel loved even when they don't deserve it. Give freely of love, truth, and hope. Speak life rather than gossip. Be loving rather than condemning. Help instead of hurt.

When a woman has this type of persona, when she's giving grace even to the people that don't deserve it from her, it is beautiful. That level of compassion, confidence, and ease is what people see from the audience as love, truth, and hope – and they describe it as graceful. Fill yourself with grace.

36: Pageant Gift Ideas for the Whole Pageant Family

WinAPageant.com/36

Pageant women love presents, both giving and receiving. As a pageant girl, I can vouch for that. The gift giving begins when you arrive for orientation, then you are showered again with gifts as you win. You give gifts to other contestants when you compete together, to your sister queens during major moments in their life like graduation and relinquishing their titles. You give gifts to your pageant directors, your parents.

Parents and directors give gifts too. When I was Miss California International, my directors gave me a gift every single day during competition week at nationals – how generous is that?

With all these opportunities for gift giving, you have to be prepared to give thoughtful gifts that will make a lasting impression and truly be remembered. I'm going to share with you some of the best gift ideas for your whole pageant family, no matter what the occasion.

Our site has links to online stores where you can get specific items from this list. That list is available at: WinAPageant.com/36.

For the New Titleholder

The best gift for the newly crowned queen is something she'll use during her year or a keepsake of her crowning moment. Gifts like car magnets, autograph cards, embroidered robes, custom luggage, and crown carrying boxes and totes are all lovely usable gifts. One of my favorite gifts from a friend of mine was a state shaped sterling silver necklace in honor of my state title. As simple, fun gifts, any crown-related item will do such as a phone case, wallet, jewelry, or cosmetics case.

For Fellow Contestants

Gift giving is common at national and international pageants when contestants arrive from all over the world. Sometimes women bring gifts representing their home state, like Florida bringing oranges,

Pennsylvania bringing Hershey's candy, and Idaho bringing potatoes (actually, I've never seen that one happen). Of course you want to get creative with how you give them. If Miss New York handed you a cheesecake right before competition that wouldn't send the right message. Put a cute poem on it, make it healthy, or find a cool way of presenting it as a specialty item.

Platform-Related Gifts

Another common gift is a small token that represents your platform, like a pin from your charitable organization or a book that you wrote.

Food Gifts

Food gifts are great as thank you gifts, especially long-distance because you can have them shipped straight from the company. One of my favorite gifts to give is Bird Pick Tea, which is a tea company in my area of southern California. I often give chocolate after a friend or client of mine competes. There are plenty of local chocolate companies that are especially classy in my area so I love spreading that joy. Food gifts are best for sharing something local with someone from out of town.

Photo Memory Gifts

Photo moments, when done in a classy way, are a great memento for any time of year. Cell phone covers, blankets, and photo frames are great for out-going royalty to give to directors, sister queens, and parents.

For Parents

Parents love to show off their kids' accomplishments. Personalized apparel is a great gift for moms, dads, and other family members. Personalized totes, aprons, or shirts with the queen's headshot on them are especially great for the parents of a junior or teen queen.

For the Out-Going Queen

When a woman is giving up her title, this is the best time to give gifts that honor her year of service. Crown display boxes or a piece of jewelry that represents her crown are beautiful gift ideas. I love custom artwork that showcases the queen in her winning gown. However, in this moment, you don't have to stick with crown-related things. You could give your queen a piece of fine jewelry like a watch or bracelet that she can wear every day in the years to come as a classy reminder of her year of service.

Of course, the best gifts are the ones that are personal to the receiver. It may be good to keep a notebook handy during your year to jot down gift ideas for those you love. In pageantry, every moment is an opportunity to give a gift.

47: Write and Record a Respectable Farewell Speech

WinAPageant.com/47

Your farewell speech is sort of your final impression. It's your opportunity to show gratitude to your team and your final moment to inspire others. It's what you want your fans and supporters to remember of your reign. It's important to make it humble, yet full of personality, gratitude, and inspiration. Plus, most women will continue to compete in this pageant system or others, so it's extra vital that you don't sound careless or ungrateful to your pageant community. Also, I don't want your farewell to be the one that everyone goes to the bathroom during or yawns and whispers through. I'm going to break down the five main components of your farewell in a beautiful outline, plus I'll share some specific advice on how to record it so you sound magnificent!

Every time you're given a microphone, it's your responsibility to make the most of it. At the end of a long year of service, sometime pageant women are so stuck on thinking of how awesome they are that they forget what this moment is truly about and how to make the most of it. As a titleholder, and as a person, really, you should always be looking for ways to honor others and shine some glorious light into the world. After all, the way to enter the gates of heaven is with gratitude.

The basic outline of an amazing farewell speech has these five main components.

1. Emotion: Feeling when winning or quote to summarize your year
2. Success: Share a success – no more than two
3. Gratitude: Thank your family, directors, and sponsors
4. Advice: Give insights to your audience, contestants, or successor
5. Sign Off: Let your personality shine and tie it back to the beginning

Step #1 – Start with a sentence or two about how you felt when you won the title. Some girls prefer to use a quote that speaks exactly what they are feeling. Just don't make it longer than a sentence.

Step #2 – Share one or two of the most impactful moments or biggest successes of your year. These should not be inside jokes, but rather things that the community can relate to and feel a part of. It's most likely that your successes can be attributed to the help and gifts of others, so honor them here and share credit with your coach, sponsors, parents, directors, and whoever else helped you along the way.

Step #3 – Show your gratitude to the people closest to you, like your family and friends. Always include the producers of the pageant here. Your role as the titleholder is as the spokesperson for the pageant, so use this time to honor the pageant itself.

Step #4 – Share a piece of advice to the audience, contestants, or your successor – not all three. Choose the one you feel most called to share insight for. Maybe you want to make a final plug for your platform or encourage the future contestants in the audience that night.

Step #5 – Giving a fun, personality-laden sign-off is a great way to bring a few smiles and tie your farewell back to the beginning to alert the audience that this is the end and they can start clapping.

In total, your speech should be no more than 3 minutes, preferable 90 seconds. Mostly because the audience will stop listening at 90 seconds, but also because you'll likely be walking and waving on stage, which, trust me, can get super awkward after 90 seconds.

Always honor your pageant team! It's likely your directors will have flowers to hand you on stage and your parents may as well, so be sure to include them in your speech. And, when their names come up, acknowledge that you wrote that, said it, and still agree with it. Please do not just walk and wave like you had nothing to do with the words being heard. It's okay to point, smile, giggle, and connect with your audience. In fact, it's human and will help maintain their attention.

Avoid complex inside jokes as it will only confuse your audience and make them feel disconnected from you.

Once you have it all written, you've got to record it. This matters just as much as the content. Excellent audio is vital for your message to be impactful.

If you aren't tech savvy, you could have a local radio DJ or your computer science friend help you. Sometimes your directors or producers of the pageant will have this all worked out. My directors at Miss California had me record it and then they edited in the music and made it sound great. If this isn't an option for you, you'll want to be prepared with your own copy. It's easier than you think. I'll walk you through it now.

First, always record your farewell speech with an excellent microphone so you avoid echoes, background fuzz, and hollow-sounding audio. You can get an inexpensive mic on Amazon, or even use your IPhone headset to plug in to record. I record audio with a free computer software program called Audacity, which also allows you to upload music with the voiceover.

Here's how you do it. Open Audacity, record your voice over, and add your music. Move the voice to start at two seconds into the music playing and lower the music volume to 20% volume or lower. With the music at that level, you don't need a fade in or out.

Remember, this is your final impression and you want to leave the audience feeling warm and fuzzy about you. You want them saying kind things as they leave the pageant that night like, "Wow, the outgoing queen is really a class-act. She's one I'd like to hire!" Or "I love the girl who gave up her title tonight. She was an incredible representative." This is the substance that winners are made of.

CHAPTER 12

ADDITIONAL RESOURCES

40: Pageant Basics and a Brief Pageant History

A pageant is a competition resulting in a crown and title. They are subjective, which is good and bad. Good because it actually makes sense to be judging people subjectively from the whole spirit of the person that they're bringing. Bad because it's not clear who receives points and for what. An objective competition is one where the person with the most points wins, like a basketball game. But in pageantry, it's not so obvious. It's subjectively based on the opinions of the judges.

The stages of competition vary, though most pageants include a gown competition and an interview portion (whether on stage or private interview). Other common areas of competition include fitness, talent, fun fashion, photogenic, casual wear, on stage modeling, and the list can go on from there. The winner commits to a year of service to the pageant as an ambassador.

Now that you know all the possibilities of what's involved, let me break down some additional pageant lingo.

There are several different groups of pageants. We call them *systems* in the industry. For example, Miss America is a pageant system; USA, international, Miss Galaxy, national American Miss, American Teenager, Miss World, Miss Earth. There are countless pageants throughout the world for every group of people imaginable. There are pageants for babies, senior citizens, men, women who use wheelchairs, petite women, married women, pre-teens, and many more categories of people.

Each pageant system can be broken down into various divisions. Divisions represent categories of competitors, usually divided by age range or marital status. For example, little miss, junior miss, teen, Miss, Ms. and Mrs. Each system has a different set of divisions, and sometimes they even call them different names.

Now that you have a basic understanding of what defines a "pageant," let's take a journey through time back to the first pageant queen ever.

Around 470 BC, there was some major political turmoil going on in Persia and the Jewish people were being persecuted. The King of the land was looking for a new Queen. He invited all of the women in his kingdom to come to his castle to march around so he could pick his favorite to be his wife (the King, I imagine, was not really a prince charming, but was more of a Jafar). Esther, a Jewish woman, was among the contestants. Her uncle helped her prepare and encouraged her to use the title of Queen to soften the King's heart and save her people from persecution. She saw this as her opportunity to position herself to make an impact.

When she showed up for the pageant, she knew she had a calling that was bigger than her alone; she was called to save her people. The King saw her beauty. He fell head over heels for her and, through a long process of dinner parties and continued phases of competition, the King finally chose Esther to be his Queen and she moved into the castle. It probably felt nice to move from persecution to a castle, but the story talks about how she was terrified of the King. She needed encouragement from others to stick with the strategy, the vision, and the goal.

As they sometimes do, things got worse before they got better, but Esther had tenacity and when the time was right, she was able to speak out on behalf of the Jewish people to the King. In the end, she saved an entire nation of people from genocide – all because she won this pageant and was given a platform where her voice could be heard.

Flash forward to somewhat more modern days. In 1839, there was a pageant held at a jousting tournament for what was called the Queen of Beauty. Then in 1921, the first Miss America pageant was held. Miss America brought local newspaper beauty contestants to Atlantic City, New Jersey. The goal was to increase tourism to the city and it worked! There were over 100,000 people that attended this very first pageant. A 16-year-old girl, Margaret Gorman, from Washington, DC was crowned and won $100. Today, Miss America is different in many ways, including the amount of the scholarship dollars awarded, which now rings it at around $20,000.

In 1952, there was a pageant called Bathing Beauty spearheaded by Catalina Swimwear in Long Beach, California. This pageant grew into the Miss USA and Miss Universe Organization pageants.

Since the 1950's, many pageants have developed as non-profit, not-for-profit, and for-profit organizations. They continue to empower women and celebrate beauty around the world.

54: Answers to Your Pageant Questions

WinAPageant.com/54

Every so often, I do question-answer sessions on Facebook. The following is a list of questions and answers I gave during one of these sessions. I wanted to include them for you here because I think they could be helpful to you. If you'd like to have your question answered, like our Facebook page at Facebook.com/WinAPageant to be alerted of future Q&A sessions.

Question #1 – What are the best colors for interview outfits?

Interview is usually done up close and personal, so solid colors that are easy on the eyes are best. If you walk in wearing a florescent bright, flowery patterned dress, it may be really difficult to focus in on what you're trying to say. My preference is for solid colors or color blocking, but there is no perfect answer for this. Choose a color that compliments your skin tone, hair, eyes, and brand.

Question #2 – Do I have to wear those nude tippy tops for swimwear?

Chinese Laundry has a famous shoe that's called the tippy top. They're nude colored patent leather so they go with everything. The answer is no. You don't have to wear anything that anyone else wears just because they are wearing it. You can wear whatever is comfortable and flattering on you.

Question #3 – Does it matter if I wear shiny or matte shoes for interview?

I recommend wearing whichever makes the most sense with the rest of your outfit. It doesn't matter which you wear, but I'd ask your stylist to stay up to date on current fashion trends. Just remember, how you speak in your interview will always overshadow the details of your outfit.

Question #4 – Is it okay to have my evening gown not quite touch the floor?

The most common style is to have the gown touch the floor when standing still and then as you walk, the hem allows the foot to peek through. That's not to say you can't have a shorter gown but it's not recommended unless you know you're going for that look.

Question #5 – If I am competing in the same pageant two years in a row, can I wear the same dress or fun fashion or other wardrobe?

Yes, you can. However, I'd invite you to consider if this wardrobe truly is the best for you. Maybe you didn't win because the wardrobe you chose isn't flattering or it may not be congruent with your brand. If you feel like it expresses the new you, one year wiser, one year smarter, and one year better, then go for it. Also, I want you to know a general fashion rule is that you wouldn't wear the same dress on the red carpet twice, so you may want to consider a different evening gown.

Question #6 – Do I have to get hair extensions?

No, you don't have to get hair extensions. Extensions are just an enhancement of the hair you have. They make it have more body or length, but most professional stylists do a great job of creating a beautiful look with or without extensions.

Question #7 – What kind of makeup should I use?

I'm not a makeup artist, but I can recommend several that will give you lessons and know what's what in the makeup world. I'd recommend getting a private lesson to choose the brands, shades, and styles that work best for your specific face.

Question #8 – What are good snacks to have back stage during my pageant?

I love to cut up an apple for backstage because it's juicy and easy to eat without messing up my teeth or makeup. Almonds and crackers are popular because they're filling, but I don't like that they dry out my mouth. Either way, bring a toothbrush, your lip makeup, liner, and gloss backstage so you can touch up after a snack.

Question #9 – How can I avoid or treat blisters at the pageant?

There's this incredible product by Band Aid brand called Blister Block. You can rub it on your feet during rehearsals and it covers your skin with wax that allows you shoe to slide on top of instead of rubbing on your skin. Another great tip is to not have your calluses removed from your feet when you get your pre-pageant pedicure. Your calluses will protect your feet when you need it most during pageant week.

Question #10 – Other than watching the news, are there any great resources for catching up on current events?

I'd suggest watching Snapchat's news channels or signing up for text alerts from CNN or Fox. When something major happens in the world, CNN will text you. That's actually how I was alerted about Michael Jackson's death. Personally, I believe you should have a general knowledge of what's going on in the world, but in pageantry you don't need to try to know everything. You're never going to know everything about everything.

Join our Facebook page to get you questions answered in future Q&A sessions: Facebook.com/WinAPageant.

82: These Women Are Ready To Win (Game Plan)

WinAPageant.com/82

I'm gushing at the seams from how proud I am of the women in the Pageant Interview Game Plan (Interview.WinAPageant.com). They are so dedicated to their success, both winning their pageant and influencing their community in such a powerful way.

The Pageant Interview Game Plan is an online course I first launched in 2016 to help women prepare for their pageant interview in just four weeks. The program consists of four modules: Set Your Foundation, Plan Your Answers, Prepare to Dazzle, and Game Day: Showtime! These are the four steps that must be followed to be fully prepared to knock the socks off your judges and nail your pageant interview. Each module is broken up into individual lessons that have homework for each one to get you further down the path to success. It's designed to allow you to finish one module every week.

Some of the women are flying through it much faster than expected and others are taking their time to allow it to soak in a little deeper. Either way is fine because when you join, you have on-going access to it, so there's really no time limit except for when you have to compete.

It comes with a Play Book that serves as a guide to get to know yourself, clarify your mission, research what the pageant is looking for, determine your stance on controversial issues, and tons of stuff that will transport you easily from confusion to clarity.

It also comes with access to a private group on Facebook that is only open to members of the course. This is where I get to see all the magic happening! Every weekday, I jump into the Facebook Group and get to answer questions to help my students excel in the program. They are really keeping me busy by taking advantage of this personal coaching opportunity.

I wanted to share with you some of what is happening in there so you could see if this is a community that may help you with your pageant interview.

Testimonial #1 – Samantha said, "I'm competing in Miss Arizona USA this weekend! Soooo thankful for this coaching. I feel so prepared and confident."

Testimonial #2 – Courtney competed just three weeks after she got into the program. She shared gratitude for her supporters and said, "To my coach, Alycia Darby, without her services I would have walked into that interview still and awkward. You let me be myself and I can't wait to train even harder this year so we bring that crown home! Thank you for believing in me." Courtney is a model and rock star with her platform. She's providing so much nourishment to the other women in the group. Everyone knows her by now.

Testimonial #3 – Rita is a computer science major and recently interviewed with Microsoft. She said, "Who would've thought that pageant interview prep would have helped me with my first round of interviews with Microsoft?!" It was all about personality and she knew herself well enough that she could confidently speak about herself even to a Microsoft hiring manager.

Testimonial #4 – Caitlen competed two weeks into the course and finished as first runner-up. Afterward, she posted a picture of her stunning interview outfit and willingly shared all the details of where she got it all. She wrote, "I placed 1st runner up at the Miss Oregon USA pageant. Alycia's interview game plan works! I felt so confident going into my interview. Thank you again."

Testimonial #5 – Angie and her teen daughter Emily are in the Game Plan. When Emily was competing this weekend, her mom was posting photos for us to be able to cheer her on. Her mom wrote, "Emily had an outstanding interview! She said the judges were sad that the time was up and she made them laugh. I think that's a good sign!" You're right, Angie that is a great sign!!

With my programs, you always get more than what you pay for. I love presents, surprises, and treats so I promise to over-deliver. In the case of the Pageant Interview Game Plan, I have a ton of bonus trainings to help with other areas of competition as well. For example, the wardrobe style guide breaks down how to define your personal style and what to wear in the interview room.

There's also a training that shows you how to stand, pose, and move on stage to model your gown, active-wear, and swimsuit.

When you join the Pageant Interview Game Plan, you have the option to get a Mock Interview with me over Skype. I record the interviews so you can watch them back and give yourself feedback.

Amanda came to her interview completely prepared in hair, makeup, and accessories. I wouldn't have been surprised if she was wearing her heels too. She's an A-player, for sure. At the end of the mock interview, I always give an assignment, and Amanda literally finished her assignment within 30 minutes and posted it in the group for immediate feedback. With that speed of implementation, she's going to be a huge success.

I'd like to invite you to look deeper into the Pageant Interview Game Plan. The program is the perfect next step after reading this book. You are poised for success and positioned to win. Take a leap of faith by investing in you and achieving your dreams.

To learn more about the details of what's included in the Pageant Interview Game Plan, and a description of all the bonus trainings and how to join, visit Interview.WinApageant.com.

ACKNOWLEDGMENTS

This book would not be possible if it weren't for these special people. I want to acknowledge them for their contributions...

My husband, Randy, for his unwavering support of our big-picture life vision and for showing me love in all my favorite ways. My all of my clients, for inspiring my creativity, fueling my mission to serve, and putting my advice to action. To the specific clients I've mentioned in this book and on the podcast for always seeking to serve and share your heart with others. To the listeners of the Win A Pageant podcast on iTunes, for motivating my continued study of pageantry and joining me weekly for our chats. To my former pageant directors, coaches and mentors, for inspiring greatness in me and encouraging my spark to light the world. To my Lord and Savior, Jesus Christ, for inspiring this dream and making my path straight.

ABOUT THE AUTHOR

Alycia Darby Zimnoch is the host of the iTunes #1 Pageant Podcast, Win A Pageant and creator of the Pageant Interview Game Plan, a 4-week online course to help women gain confidence in their pageant interview. Alycia has competed across the United States in several major pageant systems, holding two state titles. Throughout her career, Alycia has been a college professor, international spokesperson, TV host, and fitness model. She is now a pageant coach, show host, and professional speaker who can solve a Rubik's cube and moonwalk (but not at the same time). Alycia Darby lives in San Diego with her husband Randy and a beautiful view of the ocean.

Beauty,
Truth & Grace

Get More
Training
from Alycia

1. Subscribe on iTunes for
Weekly Pageant Podcasts:
WinAPageant.com/iTunes

2. Subscribe on YouTube for
Trainings and Titleholder Interviews:
WinAPageant.com/YouTube

3. Join Alycia's Pageant Training Program:
Interview.WinAPageant.com

Take the Next Step to
Win Your Pageant

Pageant Interview Game Plan

In this online course, you'll learn how to prepare your paperwork, define your pageant brand, connect with your judges and confidently communicate in your pageant interview. With one payment, you'll have lifetime access to the course and lots of additional bonus training, personalized coaching, and community.

Learn More at:
Interview.WinAPageant.com